INTRODUCING
Hegel

Lloyd Spencer • Andrzej Krauze

Edited by Richard Appignanesi

Icon Books UK   Totem Books USA

This edition published in the UK
in 2006 by Icon Books Ltd.,
The Old Dairy, Brook Road,
Thriplow, Cambridge SG8 7RG
email: info@iconbooks.co.uk
www.introducingbooks.com

Sold in the UK, Europe, South Africa
and Asia by Faber and Faber Ltd.,
3 Queen Square, London WC1N 3AU
or their agents

Distributed in the UK, Europe, South
Africa and Asia by TBS Ltd., TBS
Distribution Centre, Colchester Road,
Frating Green, Colchester CO7 7DW

This edition published in Australia
in 2006 by Allen & Unwin Pty. Ltd.,
PO Box 8500, 83 Alexander Street,
Crows Nest, NSW 2065

Previously published in the UK
and Australia in 1996 under the
title *Hegel for Beginners* and
in 1999 as *Introducing Hegel*

Reprinted 1997

This edition published in the USA
in 2006 by Totem Books
Inquiries to Icon Books Ltd.,
The Old Dairy, Brook Road,
Thriplow, Cambridge
SG8 7RG, UK

Distributed to the trade in the USA by
National Book Network Inc.,
4720 Boston Way, Lanham,
Maryland 20706

Distributed in Canada by
Penguin Books Canada,
90 Eglinton Avenue East, Suite 700,
Toronto, Ontario M4P 2YE

ISBN-10: 1-84046-785-1
ISBN-13: 978-1840467-85-7

Originating editor: Richard Appignanesi

Printed and bound in Singapore
by Tien Wah Press

Hegel is a philosopher of awe-inspiring, monumental ambition. His philosophy aims to incorporate the history of all previous philosophies. He conceives of this entire history as a process of **completion**, as all of existence, indeed the cosmos itself, evolves to full self-consciousness.

There is no room in Hegel's philosophy for a God outside or beyond the universe. His system presents itself not only as the self-consciousness of the cosmos, as Absolute Knowledge, but at the same time as an expression of the thoughts of God.

I believe that in the course of my own development as a philosopher, I have recapitulated and given expression to the "autobiography" of the Absolute.

The Life

On 27 August 1770, Georg Wilhelm Friedrich Hegel was born at No. 53 Eberhardstrasse in Stuttgart.

Hegel's father, Georg Ludwig, was a minor civil servant at the court of the Duchy of Württemberg. This area (Swabia) produced a surprising array of outstanding writers, philosophers and theologians. Hegel kept his broad sing-song Swabian inflection even when teaching at the University of Berlin.

Hegel was the eldest of three children. His younger brother, also named Georg Ludwig, became an army officer, participated in Napoleon's Russian campaign and died young.

Hegel's mother began his education in Latin before he went to school. She died when Hegel was just 11.

Hegel appears to have kept on good terms with his father, until his student days, when his enthusiasm for the French Revolution opened up a rift between father and son.

Hegel's Sister, Christiane

Hegel was very attached to his sister, Christiane. When Hegel set out his ideas on ethics, he did so by referring to Sophocles' tragedy **Antigone**.

From it, I drew the lesson that a sister's love for a brother is the highest kind of love there is.

Christiane nursed a fierce attachment to her brother. After Hegel's marriage (at age 40), Christiane suffered what Hegel would later call "hysteria" and had to resign from her post as governess. In 1820, she was committed to an asylum, but was released the following year. Troubled by bitterness over alleged wrongs, she gave vent to her jealousy of Hegel's young wife.

Foreseeing Psychotherapy?

Hegel suggested that therapy had to be dialectical: it had to involve sympathizing with the patient's complaints, winning the trust of the disturbed. It would involve respecting the patient's rational personality while at the same time overcoming the one-sidedness and abstraction of the patient's "fixed ideas".

> But I also considered having Christiane treated by the French psychiatric reformer Philippe Pinel, whose new ideas had impressed me.

Philippe Pinel (1745-1826) came to prominence during the French Revolution as the liberator of the mad.

Two weeks after Hegel's death, Christiane wrote a courteous, formal letter to his widow and included a brief memoir of her brother's childhood in which she portrayed Hegel as a precocious and industrious schoolboy.

"Lacked all bodily agility. Must have been easy to get along with, for he always had many friends; loved to jump, but was utterly awkward in dancing lessons."

Within three months of her brother's death, Christiane went out for a walk and drowned herself.

Hegel's Education

Hegel gained a thorough grounding in the classics and was fluent in Latin and Greek. The Greek tragedies were his favourite reading matter. He was at home in German literature. His scientific training, too, was good for the times.

My teachers received no salary and were dependent on fees. They attempted to maximize class sizes (even 60 or more) of varying ages and abilities.

This may have been the origin of the belief Hegel later expressed in the necessity of active and independent learning.

The Excerpt Mill

Early on and throughout his life, Hegel recorded everything he studied. Aged fifteen, he began a diary (not of personal matters but of his studies and findings).

I developed a "method of excerpting and abstracting" and wrote out (or summarized) long passages in notebooks ... I wanted to absorb everything!

Everything was grist to his "excerpt mill" — philology and literary history, aesthetics, aphorisms and witticisms, "experiences and physiognomics", mathematics, physics, psychology, pedagogy and, of course, philosophy. Hegel was already intellectually omnivorous. He wanted to absorb simply **everything**.

If, as is the case, the majority of quotations in Hegel's mature works contain mistakes or are mistakenly attributed, this is because Hegel almost always quotes from memory. The range of material he had "internalized" is staggering.

Germany in Hegel's time was a patchwork of tiny states (such as the Duchy of Württemberg where Hegel was born). There were no cities of any size and very little industry. In Prussia, serfdom was abolished, and the Jews emancipated, only after defeat by Napoleon. In 1765, James Hargreaves introduced the Spinning Jenny to England, but at the time of Hegel's birth, Germany's industrialization still lay in the future. (The first German railway opened in 1835 — four years after Hegel's death.)

Born

1749 — Johann Wolfgang von Goethe (d. 1832)

1759 — Friedrich Schiller (d. 1805)

1762 — Johann Fichte (d. 1814)

1767 — A.W. Schlegel (d. 1845)

1769 — Napoleon Bonaparte (d. 1821)

Born in 1770:

— Hegel (d. 1831)

— Friedrich Hölderlin (a poet and Hegel's closest friend during their student years) (d. 1843)

— Ludwig van Beethoven (d. 1827)

— William Wordsworth (d. 1850)

Born after 1770:

1772 — F. Schlegel (d. 1829), Novalis (d. 1801) and Samuel Taylor Coleridge (d. 1834)

1774 — Caspar David Friedrich (d. 1840)

1775 — J.M.W. Turner (d. 1851)

Events

1770 — Marie Antoinette married the Dauphin of France and James Cook was sailing around the world on his way to discovering Australia

1774 — Goethe's first novel, ***The Sorrows of the Young Werther,*** appeared

Meanwhile in America (and initiating events which would have a huge impact on the politics of Europe):

1770 — the Boston Massacre by British troops in the American colony anticipated the War of Independence (which began in 1775)

1776 — the U.S. Declaration of Independence

By the time Hegel died in 1831, the United States was an independent republic reaching across the continent to the Western ocean, and Karl Marx was 13.

A Student in Tübingen

In 1788, Hegel was enrolled as a student in the Protestant theological foundation (or *Stift*) at the University of Tübingen, in training to become a Lutheran pastor.

I was sociable and enjoyed a drink with the other students.

We found him old-fashioned in his dress, a little ponderous in his manner, and nick-named him "the Old Man".

Hegel roomed together in a loft with **Friedrich Hölderlin** (1770-1843) who became his closest friend. Even as a student, Hölderlin began to prove his poetic genius and was soon to earn the friendship and recognition of the great lights of German literature, Schiller and Goethe.

Hölderlin and Schelling

During the first years of their intense friendship, Hegel absorbed from Hölderlin an idealization of the ancient Greeks and a belief that only poetry could heal the rift that had grown up between Religion and Reason.

Unfortunately, I'm no poet!

Hegel and Hölderlin were befriended by **Friedrich Schelling** (1775-1854), son of a learned Lutheran pastor, five years younger than both of them, and already showing signs of being a philosophical boy-wonder. He had been admitted at the age of fifteen to the *Stift* at Tübingen.

Hegel's Reading

Hegel's teachers at the theological seminary noted the amount of time he devoted to philosophy. Hegel's knowledge of the Greeks was profound.

Speculations about Being among the pre-Socratics, Plato's doctrine of ideas (as being more real than appearances) and neo-Platonic ideas about *Nous* or Spirit — these seem to us to offer profound, if often obscure, answers to metaphysical questions.

Hegel's favourite reading at the time was the French Enlightenment writer **Jean-Jacques Rousseau** (1712-78). He also read all of the great literary works and essays of **J.W. von Goethe** (1749-1832) and **F. Schiller** (1759-1805) as they appeared.

The Example of Goethe

Goethe's works, and charismatic personality, had a profound influence on Hegel's whole generation. As he produced masterpiece after masterpiece, each one in a new genre, sometimes inventing genres and opening out onto a new view of the world, Goethe appeared to be making and remaking himself anew.

He was *Bildung* (education, culture and development) personified.

Hegel's admiration for and identification with Goethe was enduring. After Hegel had left university, he and Goethe corresponded and he visited Goethe frequently. In 1825, Hegel wrote to Goethe from Berlin:

my inward nature received from you nourishment and strength to resist abstraction and set its course by your images as by signal fires...

...When I survey the course of my spiritual development, I see you everywhere woven into it and would like to call myself one of your sons...

15

The French Revolution

In 1789, just before Hegel's 19th birthday, news of the fall of the Bastille and the events of the **French Revolution** reverberated around Europe. When a bunch of French — and francophile — students formed a "Political Club", Hegel joined in order to involve himself in their enthusiastic discussions about the ethical rebirth of Europe after the **Declaration of Human Rights**. One of the ringleaders, Wetzel, fled to Strasbourg to escape official censure.

Hegel and the Spirit of '89

Bliss was it in that dawn to be alive,
But to be young was very heaven.

William Wordsworth (1770-1850) (same age as Hegel)

One Sunday morning, in the spring of 1791, Hegel joined the young enthusiasts of freedom when they went out to a meadow just outside Tübingen to plant a liberty tree, singing the **Marseillaise** and reciting Schiller's **Ode to Joy** (later used by Beethoven in the 9th Symphony).

Schelling and another associate were very nearly forced to leave because they had translated the *Marseillaise*. The authorities kept a surveillance file on Hölderlin's activities.

Both the authorities who had paid for his training as a pastor, and his pious mother, to whom he was very close, expected him to settle down to a life of conventional religious service.

Absolute Freedom and the Terror

Throughout his life, Hegel celebrated Bastille Day. Freedom remained a central concern of Hegel's thought. In later years, he recalled the "spirit of '89".

All thinking beings shared in the jubilation of this epoch.

But even in his youth, Hegel was hostile to the brutal excesses of the Jacobins. In a letter to Schelling, at Christmas 1794, Hegel wrote:

"You will have heard that Carrière has gone to the guillotine. Do you still read French newspapers? If I remember rightly I have heard that they have been banned in Württemberg. This trial is very important and has uncovered the perfidious nature of the Robespierrites."

For Hegel, as for many of his contemporaries, the degeneration of the revolution into "absolute Fear" presented the most profound crisis of the spirit. An important section of Hegel's first major book, the **Phenomenology**, attempts to account for the Terror by explaining it as the result of Freedom asserted abstractly, something absolute, not related to the context of moral relations, or institutional arrangements.

Hegel as Private Tutor

After graduating in 1793, Hegel became a resident private tutor in the home of Carl Friedrich Steiger von Tschugg, a Berne patrician. For three years, Hegel lived with the family and taught the 7-year-old son, two daughters and another boy from Neufchatel.

Hegel felt isolated and suffered periods of intense depression.

I did not get on with my employers and was driven to find solace in solitary communion with nature.

He also found consolation in his studies and had free use of Captain Steiger's wonderful library.

The Swiss Aristocracy

There was also a political edge to Hegel's dissatisfaction. Germany itself was politically and economically backward. While in the little university town of Tübingen, Hegel's intense interest in politics remained a matter of ideals. He had little acquaintance with political realities. His stay in Berne, a Swiss city ruled by a patrician oligarchy to which his employer's family had close connections, opened his eyes. Writing to Schelling (16 April 1795) about elections to the *conseil souverain* (sovereign council), Hegel declares...

"The intrigues among cousins and aunts at our (German) princely courts are as nothing compared to the combinations here. The father nominates his son, or the son-in-law who brings in the biggest marriage portion, etc. To get to know an aristocratic constitution, you just have to spend a winter here before the Easter election."

Hegel's first-hand observations of feudal-aristocratic practices and institutions led him to concern himself with questions of constitutional law which were to remain a life-long preoccupation.

Political Economy

Hegel also began a study of classical political economy. By 1804, he was familiar with the Scottish political economists: **James Steuart** (1712-80), **Adam Ferguson** (1723-1816) and **Adam Smith** (1723-90).

Hegel's early writings show that he had gained an appreciation of modern free enterprise and market economics, and absorbed a concern with the problems involved in the development of "civil society".

I also developed a profound insight into the nature and philosophical significance of **labour**.

Outstripped by Schelling

Hegel's depression was at least in part occasioned by his doubts about his own abilities, aggravated by his attempt to master so many different areas of learning. He was not helped either by comparing what seemed like his own slow progress with the dazzling brilliance of his young friend Schelling, already busy developing an idealist philosophical standpoint.

In 1793, Schelling published *On Myth, Historical Legends, and Philosophical Dicta in the Most Ancient World*, in 1794, *On the Possibility of a Form of Philosophy in General*, in 1795, *On the Ego as Principle of Philosophy* as well as *Philosophical Letters on Dogmatism and Criticism*.

In a letter to Schelling (30 August, 1794) Hegel reflects...

Don't expect any comments from me on your work. I'm only an apprentice. I'm trying to study Fichte... My own work isn't worth talking about.

Almost a decade later Hegel would still be regarded, and to some extent regard himself, as the philosophical disciple of the brilliant young Schelling.

Early in 1796, Hölderlin became a private tutor in the home of Gontard, a banker in Frankfurt am Main. In October 1796 Hölderlin found Hegel a similar post with the Gogels in Frankfurt am Main so that they might be close to one another.

Elementary teaching may often oppress the mind, but you'll be happier instructing the boys than studying State and Church in their present condition.

The Importance of Hölderlin

Nah ist
und schwer zu fassen der Gott.
[Near at hand
and difficult to grasp is God.]

Hölderlin, *Patmos*

Even as students, Hegel and Hölderlin — inspired by their enthusiasm for ancient Greece — had dreamt of a new "popular religion", or *Volksreligion*, for the age of freedom. They formulated the catchphrase: "monotheism of reason and heart, polytheism of imagination and art".

Hölderlin's God seemed close at hand. But intense familiarity was itself a heavy burden. And he was already showing signs of instability.

Hölderlin had conceived an ecstatic passion for Susette Gontard, the young wife of his employer, who became "Diotima" in his lyrical novel *Hyperion*.

Hölderlin's achievement as a poet and a translator of Greek tragedies was so radical that it had to wait until the early 20th century, after the language-experiments of the modernists, to be fully recognized. He was a visionary for whom philosophical and religious concerns were as vital as anything strictly personal. He kept his Christian faith by incorporating a form of pantheism, influenced by Spinoza and the pre-Socratic philosophers.

I began as Schiller's disciple and protégé, and dedicated my early poetry to the same didactic, enlightening and educational function — that of a secular priest, who expounds not scripture, but philosophy.

Hölderlin's relationship to the world of the ancient Greeks was intense and personal, and it was difficult to make it conform to the kind of deliberate and public programme of "Classicism" to which Goethe and Schiller were committed. In their Weimar seclusion, Goethe and Schiller were able to insulate themselves to some extent from the tumults raging in the world outside. Hölderlin was more vulnerable. His poverty, his revolutionary sympathies and his volatile temperament meant that he remained prone to extremes of exultation and dejection.

In 1803 Schelling wrote to Hegel to say that Hölderlin had suffered a collapse and was living in reduced circumstances. He asked whether Hegel might offer Hölderlin shelter. Hegel replied that Hölderlin would not find Jena congenial. He never mentioned Hölderlin again.

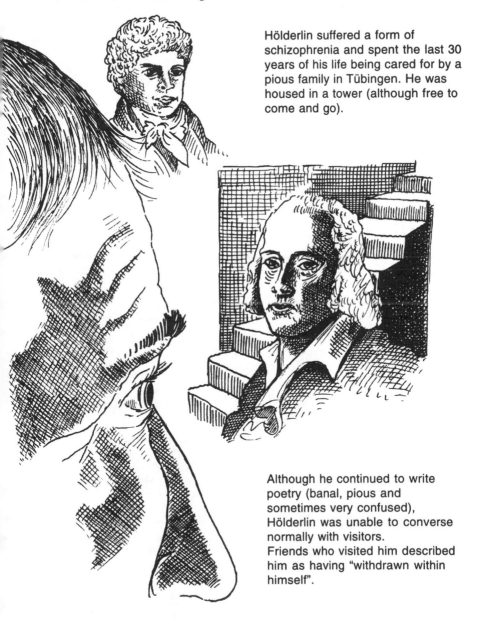

Hölderlin suffered a form of schizophrenia and spent the last 30 years of his life being cared for by a pious family in Tübingen. He was housed in a tower (although free to come and go).

Although he continued to write poetry (banal, pious and sometimes very confused), Hölderlin was unable to converse normally with visitors.
Friends who visited him described him as having "withdrawn within himself".

Was Hegel simply indifferent? Hard-hearted? Something much more profoundly traumatic was involved for him — a losing of oneself, diremption, a going within oneself, a division against the self. Hegel may have been terrified — his sister later succumbed to her own form of schizophrenia — but he can hardly have been indifferent.

I sought to make amends in the only way I could. My philosophy includes a schizophrenic principle of self-division, negation, contradiction, but its ultimate aim — like that of Hölderlin — is one of reconciliation and harmony.

Encouraged by Hölderlin, Hegel had begun serious study of the works of Immanuel Kant. He also bought and began to study Fichte's answer to Kant: the **Science of Knowledge** (**Wissenschaftslehre**) (1794).

Introducing Kant

"Our German philosophy is really but the dream of the French Revolution... Kant is our Robespierre."

Heinrich Heine

According to its enthusiasts, the French Revolution had proclaimed the good news that despite centuries of the enslavement of one man by another, and one class by another, the age of Freedom at last lay ahead.

The principle at the heart of Christian teaching is that "all men **should** be free". The French Revolution had shown that freedom was at last a real political possibility.

Freedom was announced as something universal and indivisible, as something, at least in principle, attainable by all.

And Truth was no longer an unattainable ideal either... after the three *Critiques* of **Immanuel Kant** (1724-1804).

The 3 Critiques

Kant claimed that his "critical philosophy" effected a "Copernican revolution in philosophy". In the charged atmosphere of the time, his philosophy was widely seen as corresponding to the momentous political revolution in France.

* The *Critique of Pure Reason* (1781) treated the question of how reliable or scientific knowledge is possible (or how we can know the "True").

* The *Critique of Practical Reason* (1786) sets out Kant's ethics, his understanding of moral knowledge (or how we can know the "Good").

* The *Critique of Judgement*, published in 1790, addressed questions of aesthetics and our responses to art and to natural beauty (or how we can know the "Beautiful").

From the Kantian system and its completion I expect a revolution in Germany.

Kant is the Moses of our nation.

Hölderlin

Hegel

Kant had led his people out of (philosophical) bondage; others must take them into the Promised Land.

In order to provide a solid foundation for the advancement of scientific knowledge, Kant's *Critique of Pure* (or Theoretical) *Reason* addressed a series of problems about knowledge: How do we know what we know? How is knowledge possible? What can we know? and What can we never expect to know?

31

Kant had attempted to purge philosophy of its metaphysical delusions; and metaphysics, he said, is no more than "the Idea of science as a system". In metaphysics, as in logic, we can achieve a sense of wholeness, of completeness; but — according to Kant — in metaphysics this wholeness must remain delusory, a fiction ("*eine blosse Erdichtung*").

As a result of my systematic clearing away of all previous metaphysical confusions, Truth is now a goal which might well be attained before the end of the 18th century.

The *Critique of Pure Reason* concludes with a vision of the readers advancing along "the critical path" (and thus "making it a high-road") towards Truth, towards that fulfilment which "many centuries have not been able to accomplish".

A Schizophrenia in Philosophy

Kant's split between the **Subject** of knowledge (the knower) and the **Object** of knowledge (the known) reproduces itself within the Subject itself.

His treatment of human faculties in the three *Critiques* only serves to emphasize the split between the realms of knowledge and the realms of freedom.

Fichte, Schelling, and then Hegel, all sought to carry Kant's revolution forward. Each sought in his own way to heal the divisions which Kant had enshrined in his writings: divisions between faith and reason, between Church and State, between the infinite and the finite. Each in turn sought to resolve the paradoxes which Kant had bequeathed them by re-weaving Kant's categories into a new, seamless, system.

Church and State

Let's take the position on Church and State, a split "healed" by the model of the Greek city state.

According to Kant:

> The two of them, Church and State, ought to leave each other alone; they have no business interfering with each other.

Hegel, on the contrary, believed that:

> A human being must not be split into discrete political and religious beings. Church and State cannot be separated.

For the Greeks, the *polis* — the city community — was more than a home, it was a kind of religion, the basis of all ethical commitment. But for Greek democracy, slavery was indispensible.

The Christian Religion

Hegel's first complete essay was a *Life of Jesus* in which everything miraculous or supernatural is stripped away and Jesus is made to formulate his teachings in words that make him sound remarkably like that university professor and author of the *Critique of Practical Reason*, Immanuel Kant, in accordance with Kant's own enterprise. Kant had "translated" Jesus' injunction to "Do unto others, as you would have them do unto you" into what he termed the **Categorial Imperative**.

Act only according to a maxim by which you can at the same time will that it shall become a general law.

Hegel has Jesus say...

What you can will to be a universal law among men, valid also against yourselves, according to that maxim act.

Hegel went straight on to write ***The Positivity of Christian Religion*** (1795), which is a genuinely radical essay. Its aim is to distinguish between the living, dynamic and critical voice of Jesus and everything that is institutional in Christianity, everything dogmatic or abstract — what Hegel calls "positivity" or "the mere letter of the law". Hegel is already confronting a problem which is central to all of his thinking: the tendency of impulses that begin as critical, dynamic, liberatory to turn into their opposite.

The very laws which embody freedom and human dignity can become fetters, when no longer infused with the human spirit.

There is even the suggestion in this essay that Jesus himself may have been partly responsible for the authoritarianism which has characterized Christianity.

Hegel returned to these themes in 1799, in *The Spirit of Christianity and its Fate*, but the emphasis is dramatically altered. No longer does Hegel write as a son of the Enlightenment attempting to make Christianity acceptable to reason, but more like a Christian mystic, struggling to find adequate speculative expression for the message of Jesus.

Jesus appears as a tragic, revolutionary figure confronting the situation of degradation and oppression suffered by his people.

Jesus represents the spirit of love and is compelled to go against the dead weight of Jewish law and institutions.

Jesus is seen as infusing Judaism with the moral beauty of the Greeks. Hegel's close association with Hölderlin, "the sensitive poet who adored Greece with all the pathetic love of a Christian heart", opened up a path for Hegel.

Throughout the 1790s, Hegel's primary concerns remained religious and moral. But for Hegel such concerns were still indistinguishable from political questions. And he was equally critical of oppressive, out-of-date political institutions, or as he put it...

Positivity = "Institutions... from which the spirit has flown".

Positivity = Institutions from which the spirit has flown.

In the **First Programme for a System of German Idealism**, written jointly with Schelling (1796), Hegel expresses a radical view of the State:

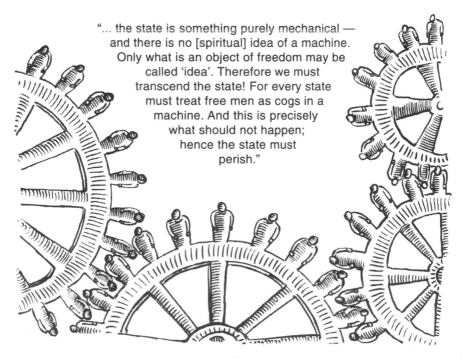

"... the state is something purely mechanical — and there is no [spiritual] idea of a machine. Only what is an object of freedom may be called 'idea'. Therefore we must transcend the state! For every state must treat free men as cogs in a machine. And this is precisely what should not happen; hence the state must perish."

Introducing Spinoza

The German idealist philosophers dreamed of a world made whole again after the cleavages introduced by Kant. One source of inspiration, and a promising model, was the greatest Rationalist of them all, **Baruch de Spinoza** (1632-77), an uncompromising monist whose vision of the universe was of a coherent whole, harmonious and transparent to reason.

Spinoza, a Dutch philosopher of Portuguese Jewish origin, was a pioneer in the contentious area of biblical criticism.

In my studies of the bible I sought to demonstrate the principle that freedom of thought is essential to social existence.

Spinoza's main work, misleadingly entitled *Ethics* (1675), in fact contains his metaphysics, together with a rationalist blueprint for the investigation of nature.

The whole book is set out in the form of a set of logical deductions, rather like Euclid's geometry. Hegel was the only other philosopher to suggest that all of his ideas could be given in something like "deductive" form.

Spinoza was a monist.

I seek to demonstrate that mind and matter, or everything spiritual (or intellectual) and everything material, are but aspects of the **same basic Substance**. This Substance is the same as God. God is the same as the universe, the totality of all things.

Spinoza's radical rationalism led him to a strong belief in a direct access to the Truth, via Reason. Like Hegel, he did not see error as something external to, and opposed to, or threatening to, Truth. "The Truth is its own measure and the measure of what is false."

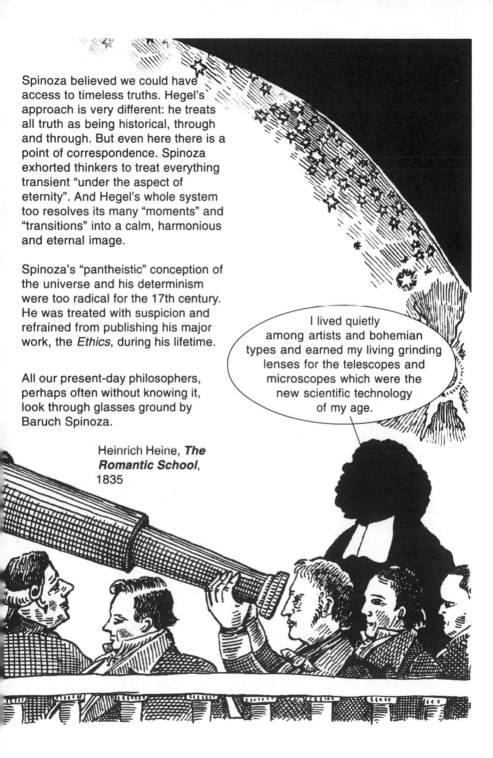

Spinoza believed we could have access to timeless truths. Hegel's approach is very different: he treats all truth as being historical, through and through. But even here there is a point of correspondence. Spinoza exhorted thinkers to treat everything transient "under the aspect of eternity". And Hegel's whole system too resolves its many "moments" and "transitions" into a calm, harmonious and eternal image.

Spinoza's "pantheistic" conception of the universe and his determinism were too radical for the 17th century. He was treated with suspicion and refrained from publishing his major work, the *Ethics*, during his lifetime.

All our present-day philosophers, perhaps often without knowing it, look through glasses ground by Baruch Spinoza.

Heinrich Heine, *The Romantic School*, 1835

I lived quietly among artists and bohemian types and earned my living grinding lenses for the telescopes and microscopes which were the new scientific technology of my age.

Introducing Fichte

In 1792, a revolutionary theological and philosophical essay was published anonymously under the provocative title, **An Attempt at a Critique of All Revelation**. Because it came from the same publisher as Kant's works, and because Kant's philosophy of religion was eagerly awaited, the public supposed that the work was his. The author was in fact the young **Johann Gottlieb Fichte** (1762-1814).

I proceeded to correct this error and to praise the real author.

With this endorsement from the great Kant, I leapt to the attention of the public.

In 1793, Fichte's writings in favour of the French Revolution earned him the reputation of being a dangerous democrat and Jacobin. Nevertheless, an endorsement from Goethe helped to get him appointed in 1794 as professor of philosophy in Jena.

This Fichte could claim to have done in his **Basis of the Entire Theory of Science (*Grundlage der gesammten Wissenschaftslehre*) (1794).**

Fichte was unrelenting in his attempts to make his philosophy clear. In 1801, he published an introduction to the *Wissenschaftslehre*, entitled **A Report, Clear as the Sun, for the General Public on the Real Essence of the Latest Philosophy: an Attempt to Compel the Reader to Understand.**

Enlightenment ...

Let's review the main features of Hegel's journey so far. Hegel belongs to a generation of German Romantic writers inspired by the radical new ideas of the Enlightenment, and yet who felt the need to reconcile these ideas with age-old philosophical traditions, as well as with religion.

French Enlightenment philosophers, such as **Diderot** and **Voltaire**, had espoused the cause of Reason against what they saw as an unholy alliance of (the Catholic) Church and State. Although several notable Enlightenment thinkers held on to some belief in a deity (and some, indeed, professed to be Christians), a strain of anti-religious sentiment runs through their polemics. The prominent role assumed by philosophy in the turmoil that led up to the French Revolution seemed to set Reason against Faith.

Germany's most eminent Enlightenment philosopher, Immanuel Kant, was hostile to metaphysics and attempted to erect an insuperable barrier between Reason and Faith. The title of one of his books proclaimed the necessity of bringing *Religion Within the Bounds of Mere Reason Alone* (1793). Such a restricted and fragmented conception of Reason could only act as a provocation.

"The contrast between faith and reason is in our time a contrast within philosophy itself."
Hegel in an essay, *Faith and Knowledge* (around 1800)

... Post-Enlightenment and German Idealism

The three most important German philosophers of the post-Enlightenment generation after Kant, the German Idealists, Fichte, Schelling and Hegel, were all trained in theology to become Lutheran pastors. Schelling and Hegel started out — and ended up — as convinced Lutherans. As Hegel liked to say...

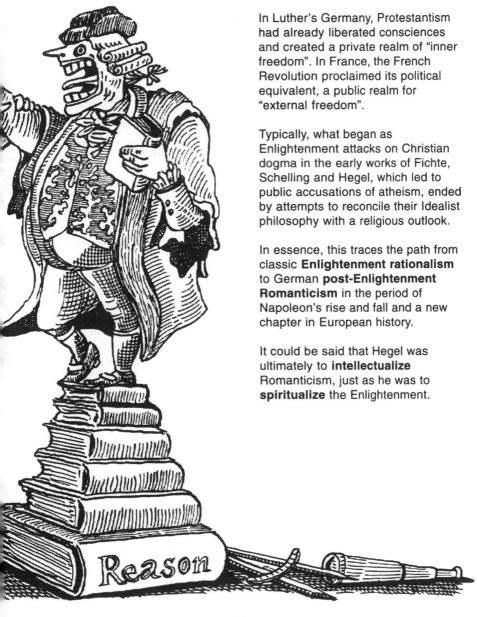

In Luther's Germany, Protestantism had already liberated consciences and created a private realm of "inner freedom". In France, the French Revolution proclaimed its political equivalent, a public realm for "external freedom".

Typically, what began as Enlightenment attacks on Christian dogma in the early works of Fichte, Schelling and Hegel, which led to public accusations of atheism, ended by attempts to reconcile their Idealist philosophy with a religious outlook.

In essence, this traces the path from classic **Enlightenment rationalism** to German **post-Enlightenment Romanticism** in the period of Napoleon's rise and fall and a new chapter in European history.

It could be said that Hegel was ultimately to **intellectualize** Romanticism, just as he was to **spiritualize** the Enlightenment.

Arrival in Jena

In 1799, Hegel's father died and left him a modest inheritance.

In January 1801, Hegel arrived in Jena, poor, inarticulate, disorganized and hitherto unsuccessful. Even with the help of his young and brilliant friend, Schelling, Hegel knew it would be a struggle to make his mark. Jena was then the capital of German philosophy, and Weimar that of German literature. Schelling, not yet 26, was already a professor at the University of Jena and had published five books.

This allowed him to lecture at the university, not on a salary, but paid out of the fees of students.

One of Hegel's antagonists pointed out that there were already nearly as many teachers as students in the faculty of philosophy — 20 to 30. In fact, there were twelve other teachers, six of them *Privatdozenten*, lecturing on philosophy.

Despite enjoying the support of men like Goethe and Schelling, Hegel did not receive an academic salary until 1807, just before he left Jena, at the age of 37.

Differences between Schelling and Fichte

The philosophic systems of Fichte and Schelling were gaining currency in German universities. Fichte eventually alienated Schelling by treating him as if he were Fichte's assistant.

Fichte believed that a philosophical system had to be founded on a single basic proposition or principle.

I developed the subjectivism inherent in Kant's "critical philosophy" by taking, as my fundamental principle, the Ego (or the "I" — *das Ich*).

By this he meant not an individual subjectivity, or ego, but the cosmos, all reality, as an **Absolute Subjectivity**.

Influenced by my readings of Spinoza, I soon abandoned Fichte's formulations in favour of a new view of the Absolute as a neutral "Identity" that underlies both the subject (the mind) and the object (nature).

Schelling cajoled Hegel into writing his first real publication, a pamphlet of just over 100 pages on the ***Difference Between the Philosophical Systems of Fichte and Schelling*** (1801). Not surprisingly, Hegel supports Schelling.

Together Schelling and Hegel collaborated on the publication of the **Critical Journal of Philosophy**, in order to take up "cudgels, whips and bats" for what Hegel referred to as "the Cause".

Schelling had developed the ideas of Kant and Fichte in an original and profound way. Many of the elements which later appear systematized in Hegel's very comprehensive system of **Absolute Idealism** are first encountered in Schelling's brilliant essays. His ability to formulate ever-new positions on important issues was not matched by an ability to do the sustained work of synthesis and elaboration called for by his (Schelling's) own philosophy.

...Schelling conducts his education in public!

In 1803 Schelling (28 years old) married Caroline Schlegel (40), after the legal dissolution of her marriage with the prominent Romantic scholar, **A.W. Schlegel** (1767-1845). The scandal was too much for Jena. Schelling was forced to move to Würzburg, where he turned to problems of religion and to the theosophical utterances of the mystical shoemaker of Görlitz, **Jakob Boehme** (1575-1624). In 1806 he moved to Munich. He was 31, the author of more than a dozen major publications, and could claim to be Germany's foremost philosopher. Hegel, to whom he had given some assistance, was 37, penniless and completely unknown.

Soon after Hegel's arrival, Jena began to lose its pre-eminent position. Fichte had been dismissed in 1799, after being accused of atheism. According to Goethe, discontent stole from mind to mind. Fichte moved to Berlin, Schiller settled in Weimar. Schelling joined fellow-academics, Hufeland and Paulus, in accepting posts at the University of Würzburg. The University of Jena was losing its most illustrious professors.

Hegel had arrived at the centre of things — only to find the centre walking away from him. "Philosophy" as Hegel was later to remark, "always arrives too late on the scene".

What I need is a major publication to set me apart and secure my academic career.

Genesis of *The Phenomenology of Spirit*

For the summer semester of 1803 Hegel announced that he would present **all philosophy as a system** and from then on he referred repeatedly to his *Primer of the Philosophical Encyclopaedia*, which was supposedly coming out in the next few weeks — but never did. Instead of a simple academic primer, it became a work of genius which would change philosophy forever.

At last, in 1806, I was able to provide my students with a printed text to accompany my lectures.

F.I. NIETHAMMER

These were the proof sheets of his first real book, the **System of Science, Part One** (the words "Phenomenology of Spirit" only appear in small print at the foot of the page). He was still working on the second half, trying to meet a deadline of 18 October. His friend, Niethammer, had guaranteed payment if Hegel failed to meet his publisher's deadline. He urged Hegel to join him in Bamberg, Bavaria, if the corrected manuscript could not be posted by 13 October.

Napoleon Advances

Napoleon had been in control of much of southern Germany for some time. Now his armies were closing in on Prussia and the last remnants of the Holy Roman Empire.

Hegel rushed the final chapters of his book, aware of an intersection between Hegelian philosophy and world history. The sole copy of a part of the manuscript was entrusted to a courier who rode through the French lines from Jena to Bamberg on the eve of the Battle of Jena.

On the night of 12 October Napoleon bombarded Jena and the next day his troops entered the city. Hegel, still with the last sheets in his pocket, wrote to Niethammer.

"I saw the Emperor — that World Soul — riding out to reconnoitre the city; it is truly a wonderful sensation to see such an individual, concentrated here on a single point, astride a single horse, yet reaching across the world and ruling it..."

This was not a new enthusiasm. Hegel saw Napoleon as the man destined to make the positive heritage of the French Revolution a practical reality in Germany. This would involve a dissolution of feudal privilege and the establishment of the rights of citizens — in fact, a completely new political dispensation.

The pressures on Hegel came not only from Napoleon's progress and his own tangled dealings with his publisher. The wife of Hegel's landlord was pregnant with his child. Hegel's illegitimate son, Ludwig, was born on 5 February 1807.

For some time Hegel had been looking about for another academic position.

Thank God! As a result of Niethammer's influence I have been offered a post as editor of the *Bamberger Zeitung*, a Catholic daily paper.

On 20 February 1807, he wrote to Niethammer to say that he would accept the post. Meanwhile he continued to turn out page after page of the *Phenomenology of Spirit*.

What is the *Phenomenology* About?

The *Phenomenology of Spirit* is without doubt one of the strangest books ever written. Almost all of what Hegel was to develop systematically over the rest of his life is prefigured in these pages. The book speaks throughout of Reason, and claims to be tracing a set of logical deductions, but bears all the signs of having been written under inspiration.

Hegel describes it as a kind of ladder by means of which we can climb from our immediate, limited experience of the world, up to a truly philosophic vantage point. Once we have attained such a properly philosophical point of view, this ladder can be dropped or discarded. Hegel insists that the beginning of philosophy presupposes the point of view reached only at the end of the *Phenomenology*. But this ladder takes a very peculiar form. In fact, as Hegel himself notes, it is circular. Indeed, in this and later books, Hegel refers to "circles within circles".

"The Science of the Experience of Consciousness"

The German word for "experience" — *Erfahrung* — already suggests the verb "to journey", *fahren*. The *Phenomenology* records the process whereby consciousness is expanded — by means of its journey — from simple immediacy to the form of systematic science.

"The particular individual, so far as content is concerned, has also to go through the stages through which the general mind has passed, but as shapes once assumed by mind and now laid aside, as stages of a road which has been worked over and levelled out. Hence it is that, in the case of various kinds of knowledge, we find that what in former days occupied the energies of men of mature mental ability sinks to the level of information, exercises, and even pastimes, for children; and in this educational progress we can see the history of the world's culture [delineated] in faint outline."

From the *Introduction*

History as Self-Realization

This sequence of evolution is almost like a fossil record of "thought phases", modelled on phases actually experienced by humanity in the course of its history. Historical events — such as the Reformation, the French Revolution, Napoleon's conquests, and philosophical ones, such as Kant's crowning of the Enlightenment, the rise of German Idealism — feature as processes of intellectual experiment and discovery.

It is history in highly compressed form, seen as a journey of intellectual reflection and self-discovery, which has been in progress for millenia, but has only just become aware of itself as such.

Hegel's philosophy embodies the memory of humanity as it pieces together what has been left dismembered in fragments. It is humanity struggling to take possession of the totality of its own past by seeing the story of humankind's **self-realization** as a significant whole.

Hegel's recapitulated history of humanity's progress reveals how consciousness is made aware of itself, thereby transforming itself into self-consciousness — or rather, consciousness is made aware that it is **already** self-consciousness.

In order to be conscious of the world, I must at the same time be conscious of being conscious. Self-consciousness is "built in" to consciousness.

The two-way (subject/object) relation is soon complicated by the awareness that I am not alone in the world.

Consciousness of self (self-consciousness in-itself) is not yet real subjectivity.

Self-consciousness, or subjectivity, is immediately a consciousness of a **lack** of something — the object. Freedom has its beginning here, in **Desire**. Self-consciousness is consciousness aware of its own unity and purpose. But it is also consciousness divided, isolated from other consciousnesses. If humankind is to lead its history self-consciously, Hegel must show how individual self-consciousnesses can be related to one another in an essential way. He has to show how freedom can both divide, and ultimately also unite, human individuals.

The Master and the Slave

To explain this process, Hegel outlines a mythical encounter between two primeval self-consciousnesses. This is the famous example of **"the master and the slave"**.

Each self, deeply absorbed in the business of living, at first confronts the other as an obstruction to its own possession of the world and demands recognition from the other.

The result is a life-and-death struggle for recognition by the other. The self who submits, rather than face death, becomes the slave.

I have obtained **recognition**.

Yes, but not from another self — only from a being reduced to an object and a means, a slave.

There is no way for the master, on his own, to escape from his own form of dependency and alienation.

In quaking respect for the master, the slave is shaken out of narrow self-identification and self-interest.

The slave is put to work and (slowly) learns **self**-respect and comes to see himself reflected in the work of his hands.

I recognize that the world about me is the world I have made. It is my world — although we are both possessed by the master.

Paradoxically the master remains in the state of dependence while the slave (slowly) educates himself towards independence.

Desire, consciousness and self-consciousness, dread, alienation, the creation of the world as the result of oppressed labour — the true struggle in all this is shown as the struggle for **recognition**. It is no wonder that Hegel's myth continues to have such resonance to the present. Marxists, Existentialists, the intellectual architects of Negritude and the Black Consciousness movement, have all been drawn to the sombre richness of Hegel's tale. And although Hegel speaks throughout of "he", feminists, too, have found inspiration here.

14 Stations of the Cross

The journey of the *Phenomenology* can be divided into 14 stages, organized under three main headings, **Consciousness**, **Reason** and **Spirit** (or Mind). Hegel ends with the most surprising image — the **"Calvary of Absolute Spirit"**. Two paths, those of History and the Science of Knowing, meet atop the hill of Calvary on which the Absolute Spirit is being crucified. The 14 stages of consciousness can be seen as 14 Stations of the Cross.

Consciousness

1. Sense-Certainty, which starts out from the Here and Now, and deals with the This, the particular.
2. Perception (*Wahrnehmung*) which may involve deceptions, and reveals the contradictory nature of our awareness of the world.
3. The Understanding (*Verstand*) which reveals order, regularities and organization.

Self-Consciousness

4. Certainty of Self, and the struggle for recognition and for freedom.

Reason

5. Observing reason (*beobachtenden Vernunft*) which includes observation of nature and of the self (in logic and psychology).

6. Actualization (*Verwirklichung*) or putting into reality, of rational self-consciousness (*vernünftigen Selbstbewusstseins*) through its own activity (in selfish pleasure, in morality, as well as in self-conceit or self-importance).

7. Individuality satisfied in itself, including the rational formulation of laws and the rational testing of laws.

Spirit

8. True spirit or the ethical order. This section treats of human and divine law, guilt and destiny. There is material on legality, sexual relations and the family.

9. Spirit alienating or expressing itself in culture (*Bildung*). The three subdivisions treat of the Age of Faith and the Reformation, the Enlightenment, and the French Revolution and its dissolution into the Terror.

10. Morality and conscience or Spirit that is certain of itself. Here Hegel deals with the Kantian concept of duty, and with other forms of bourgeois freedom.

11. Natural Religion, including God as Light, as plant or animal and as the Creator.

12. Art, or what Hegel entitles, "Religion in the Form of Art", with a treatment of cults, and of "The Spiritual Work of Art".

13. Revealed religion in the form of the death (crucifixion) of God and the mysteries of the Holy Trinity.

14. **Absolute knowing** or **absolute knowledge** (*absoluten Wissens*)...

Absolute Knowledge...

Absolute Knowledge in Hegel's scheme of things is much the same as "philosophy as such" and coterminous with his **own** system of philosophy which has not yet been set out in fully systematic form.

In the short last chapter of the book, **Geist** (Spirit or Mind) comes to know itself. It recognizes itself in the world it has shaped and created and can grasp that "its Becoming, History, is a conscious, self-mediating process — Spirit emptied out into Time".

This Becoming presents a slow-moving succession of Spirits, a gallery of images, each of which, endowed with all the riches of Spirit, moves thus slowly just because the Self has to penetrate and digest this entire wealth of its substance.

The final chapter on "Absolute Knowing" is so short that it feels almost truncated — as if the slow-motion retracing of the path that leads up to this point has suddenly speeded up. We are back in real time — only now with a sense of our own thinking existence which reaches back over time and in it sees its pattern and purpose.

This exultant vision of Absolute Knowledge, the self-knowledge of Absolute Spirit, is arrived at only through the "seriousness, the pain, the patience and the labour of the negative". As Hegel explains: "The life of the Spirit is not the life that shrinks from death and keeps itself untouched by devastation, but rather the life that endures it and maintains itself in it. It wins truth only when, in utter dismemberment, it finds itself... Spirit is this power only by looking the negative in the face, and tarrying with it."

The *Phenomenology* offers what had already been forecast a decade before in Hegel's early attacks on conventional theology.

To embrace the whole energy of the suffering and discord that has controlled the world and all forms of its culture for some thousand years, and also to rise above it — this can be done by philosophy alone.

Hegel eloquently described his own "dark night of the soul" in a letter to K.J.H. Windischmann (1775-1839), a Catholic doctor who later became a professor of philosophy.

"... this descent into dark regions where nothing reveals itself to be fixed, definite and certain, where glimmerings of light flash everywhere but, flanked by abysses, are rather darkened in their brightness and led astray by the environment, casting false reflections far more than illumination. Each beginning of every path breaks off again and runs into the indefinite, loses itself, and wrests us away from our purpose and direction. From my own experience I know this mood of the soul, or rather of reason, which arises when it has finally made its way with interest and hunches into a chaos of appearances and, though inwardly sure of the goal, has not yet worked through them to clarity, and a detailed grasp of the whole. I have suffered a few years of this hypochondria, to the point of enervation. Probably everyone has such a turning point in his life, the nocturnal point of the contraction of his essence in which he is forced through a narrow passage by which his confidence in himself and everyday life grows in strength and assurance... It is science which has led you into this labyrinth of the soul, and science alone is capable of leading you out again and healing you."

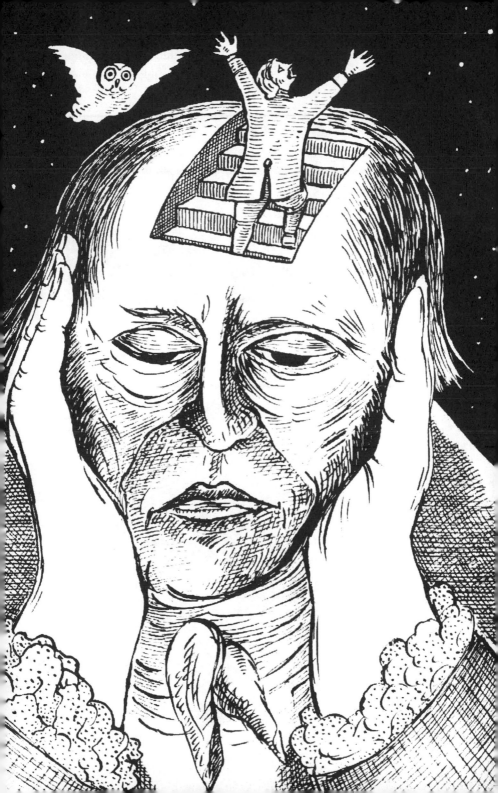

The Newspaper Editor

Napoleon's defeat of Prussia at the Battle of Jena brought all proceedings at the university to a halt.

Hegel had already begun work as editor of a Catholic daily paper in Bavaria, the *Bamberger Zeitung*. Bavaria had been under the influence of Napoleon for some time. As editor, Hegel was in close touch with day-to-day events, from the reforms in Bavaria to the news from the rest of Europe and further abroad, a position he quite obviously enjoyed. Despite his pro-Napoleonic attitudes, he had his difficulties with the censors.

Hegel goes to Nuremberg

Niethammer had been promoted to an important post in the Bavarian education office and was working to reform the education system there. He was a Protestant, ranged in this task against the old Catholic hierarchy. In his efforts to introduce an open-minded, humanistic curriculum, Niethammer drew on the French system as a model. He also enlisted Hegel to this vital political task. In 1808, Niethammer found him the post of Rector and Professor of Philosophy at the *Gymnasium*, or classical school for boys, at Nuremberg.

Hegel was appointed headmaster (or Rector) in 1808 and held the post until 1816. Altogether — as private tutor, teacher and headmaster — Hegel spent 14 years involved in teaching at secondary, rather than university, level. He certainly took his job seriously. The school had to be developed amid a lack of funds and apparatus. Hegel faced the challenge of that "all-powerful and unalterable destiny which is called the course of business".

Hegel spent a good deal of time considering methods of introducing schoolboys (14-19 years) to speculative thought in the enlarged and systematic form he was developing.

"Serious study of the ancient classics is the best introduction to philosophy. But perhaps not a road open to everyone."

Hegel's Marriage and Illegitimate Son

In 1811, aged 41, Hegel married Marie von Tucker, the daughter of a respected Nuremberg family. She was scarcely half his age.

Christiana Burkhardt, née Fischer, mother of Hegel's illegitimate child, Ludwig (b. 1807), heard of the marriage and tried to create a stir. Hegel had been paying money to support his son and appears to have placated her.

Our marriage went ahead and it was a very happy one.

In 1812 our first child, a girl, was born, but soon died.

Hegel's brother Ludwig, godfather of Hegel's illegitimate son, fell during Napoleon's Russian campaign.

When Hegel was finally offered a chair in philosophy in 1816, he arranged to have his illegitimate son brought into the family. By then, the Hegels had two other sons aged 3 and 4. Ludwig was well-educated but became bitter at not being allowed to study medicine.

For a while I associated with radical student activists, before running away from a position my father had found for me to join the military.

He was shipped to the Dutch East Indies where he caught fever and died.

Is Philosophy Teachable?

Hegel's involvement in teaching did not keep him away from his philosophical work. His most dauntingly abstract book, the **Science of Logic**, was published in three parts in 1812, 1813 and 1816.

In order for philosophy to be teachable, Hegel believed, it had to be given a regular structure.

Hegel started his pupils with the principles underlying law, morality and religion and progressed only in the higher classes to logic and philosophy. He set out a comprehensive, but highly abridged, version of his philosophical system for classroom use, the **Philosophical Propaedeutic**, only published after his death.

Hegel attempted by "graduated exercises" to introduce his pupils to speculative thought.

I would start each week's four-hour session by reading out short paragraphs, and then using the remaining time to explain at greater length, encouraging questions and discussion of the topic, and covering any difficulties, of which there were many.

Aristotelian Logic

In 1808, Hegel still talked of constructing some sort of bridge between traditional logic — set out in classical form by **Aristotle** — and his own. Aristotelian logic had been the standard for 2,000 years. Aristotle (384-322 B.C.) perfected a form of deductive argument called the **syllogism**.

3 propositions:

all men are mortal   – major premise
all Greeks are men   – minor premise
therefore, all Greeks are mortal   – conclusion

Classical reasoning assumes the principle of **logical identity**: A = A, or A is not non-A.

I can't build a bridge between this logic and my mode of thinking. I need something new!

Why did Hegel need a different logic? Perhaps you may already have seen the answer to this in Hegel's *Phenomenology*.

Hegel usually referred to the *Phenomenology* as his "psychology", because it was the only one of his writings which deals with the world, not as it appears to Absolute Mind (or Spirit) but to quite ordinary minds — like our own. It traced a path from our everyday commonsense states of mind to the vantage point of "Systematic Science".

But in writing that book, I became aware of employing a new and unprecedented way of thinking.

Dialectical Thinking

Hegel's different way of thinking has become known as **dialectical thinking**. What makes dialectical thinking so difficult to explain is that it can only be seen in practice. It is not a "method" or a set of principles, like Aristotle's, which can be simply stated and then applied to whatever subject-matter one chooses.

How do we begin to understand how this dialectic works?

First, by beginning to appreciate Hegel's unique philosophical ambition.

During our university days, Hölderlin and I shared an elusive vision of the "One in All". Can I now convey this mystical conception by means of **logic**?

Totality

For Hegel, only the whole is true. Every stage or phase or moment is partial, and therefore partially untrue. Hegel's grand idea is "**totality**" — which preserves within it each of the ideas or stages that it has overcome or subsumed. Overcoming or subsuming is a developmental **process** made up of "moments" (stages or phases). The **totality** is the **product** of that process which preserves all of its "moments" as elements in a structure, rather than as stages or phases.

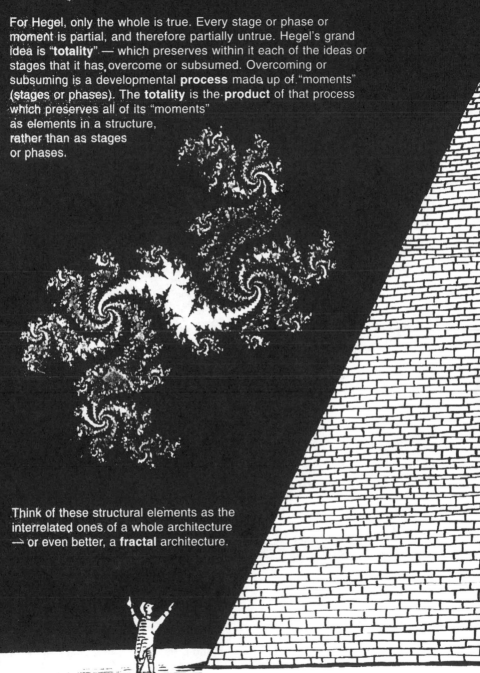

Think of these structural elements as the interrelated ones of a whole architecture — or even better, a **fractal** architecture.

Aufhebung or Sublation

Aristotle's logic is concerned with separate, discrete (self-) identities in a deductive pattern. Hegel dissolves this classical static view of logic in a dynamic movement towards the **whole**. The whole is an overcoming which preserves what it overcomes.

Nothing is lost or destroyed but raised up and preserved as in a spiral. Think of the opening of a fern or a shell.

This is an organic rather than mechanical logic. Hegel's special term for this "contradiction" of **overcoming** and at the same time **preserving** is *Aufhebung*, sometimes translated as **"sublation"**.

For anything to happen, everything has to be in place.

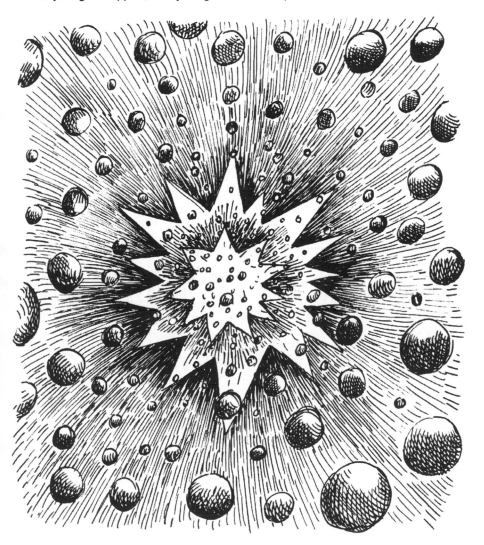

Quantum theory, postmodern cosmology, chaos theory, computer interfacing and ecology all essentially subscribe to this view of a "totality" in question, without being "Hegelian".

A Grammar of Thinking

In Hegel's treatment of logic, thinking dwells on itself, rather than trying to comprehend the world. The *Science of Logic* deals with logical categories, not the accidents of history or various modes of relating to the world. It is rather absent or distant from the world as such.

I liken my study of logic to the study of grammar. You only really see the rewards when you later come to observe language in use and you grasp what it is that makes the language of poetry so evocative.

Hegel deals with a sequence of logical categories: being, becoming, one, many, essence, existence, cause, effect, universal, mechanism, and "life". Each is examined in turn and made to reveal its own inadequacies and internal tensions. Each category is made to generate another more promising one — which in its turn will be subject to the same kind of scrutiny.

Negation

Hegel calls this dynamic aspect of his thinking the power of **"negation"**. It is by means of this "negativity" of thought that the static (or habitual) becomes discarded or dissolved, made fluid and adaptable, and recovers its eagerness to push on towards "the whole".

Dialectical thinking derives its dynamic of negation from its ability to reveal "contradictions" within almost any category or identity.

Hegel's "contradiction" does not simply mean a mechanical denial or opposition. Indeed, he challenges the classical notion of static self-identity, A = A, or A ≠ non-A.

By negation or contradiction, Hegel means a wide variety of relations — difference, opposition, reflection or relation. It can indicate the mere insufficiency of a category or its incoherence. Most dramatically, categories are sometimes shown to be self-contradictory.

Three Kinds of Contradiction

1. The three divisions of the *Science of Logic* involve three different kinds of contradiction. In the first division — **Being** — the opposed pair of concepts at first seem flatly opposed, as if they would have nothing at all to do with one another: Being — Nothing / Quantity — Quality. Only by means of analysis or deduction can they be shown to be intimately interrelated.

2. In the second division — **Essence** — the opposed pairs immediately imply one another. The Inner and the Outer, for example: to define one is at the same time to define the other.

3. In the third division — the **Concept** — we reach an altogether more sophisticated level of contradiction. Here we have concepts such as Identity whose component parts, Universality and Particularity, are conceptually interrelated.

The third level is more difficult to depict or illustrate than the others — because it is truly abstract. Here we are talking about relations which can only be disentangled from one another by process of abstraction.

For example, we can see how one of our most vital categories — **individuality** — can be built up out of a pair of apparently opposing principles, **universality** and **particularity**.

Universal = likeness, particularity = unlike, individuality = unique web of interrelations: an "individual" is thus a web of self-maintained relations, comparisons and differences.

Once we have been alerted to the significance of these terms, we become aware of what Hegel means, in his historical or political or aesthetic writings, when he uses a term such as "universal" or "particular". Throughout his writings, we see Hegel bring such terms into play as terms of judgement.

As one progresses through the stages of Hegel's *Logic*, so one advances from the levels on which knowledge is still tied to "representation" (*Vorstellung*) or image-ination, to the realms of truth itself. In the Concept, truth dispenses with any involvement with "representation" — it presents itself as pure thought, or as thought **thinking** itself. Truth proper is, in Hegel's own terms, "imageless".

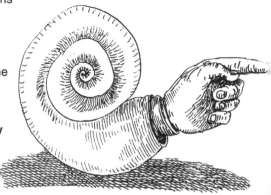

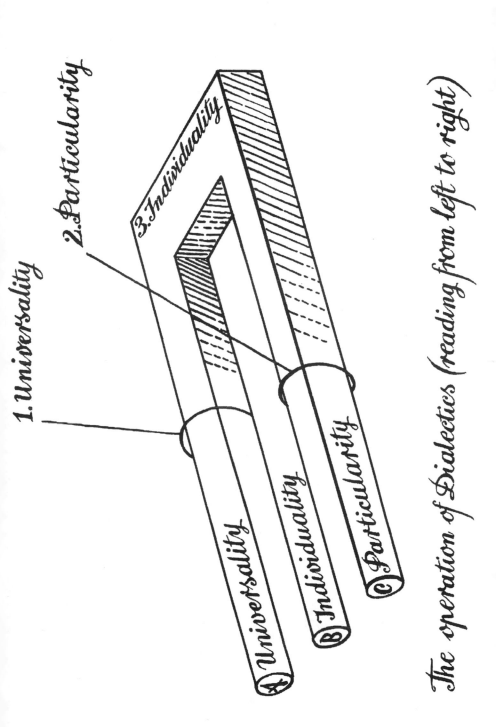

1. Universality

2. Particularity

3. Individuality

A Universality

B Individuality

C Particularity

The operation of Dialectics (reading from left to right)

Triadic Structure

If negation is the inner life-force of the dialectic, then **triadic structure** is its organic, fractal form.

THESIS ➡ **ANTITHESIS** ➡ **SYNTHESIS**

A thought is affirmed which on reflection proves itself unsatisfactory, incomplete or contradictory...

which propels the affirmation of its negation, the **anti**-thesis, which also on reflection proves inadequate...

and so is again negated...

In classical logic, this double negation ("A is not non-A") would simply reinstate the original thesis. The synthesis does not do this. It has "overcome and preserved" (or sublated) the stages of the thesis and antithesis to emerge as a higher rational unity.

Note: This formulation of Hegel's triadic logic is convenient, but it must be emphasized that he **never** used the terms thesis, antithesis and synthesis.

Hegel's dialectic triad also serves another logical purpose. Kant had distinguished two kinds of logic.

1. The **analytic** logic of understanding which focusses the data of sense-experience to yield knowledge of the natural **phenomenal** world.

2. The **dialectic** logic of understanding which operates independently of sense-experience and **erroneously** professes to give knowledge of the **transcendent noumena** ("things in themselves" or also the "infinite" or the "whole").

Hegel's view is completely different.

1. Analytic understanding is only adequate for natural science and practical everyday life, not for philosophy.

2. Dialectic reason is not concerned with Kant's "transcendent", nor with the abstract "mutilated" parts of reality, but with reality as a **totality**, and therefore gives **true** knowledge.

What is Knowing?

Knowing, for Hegel, is something you **do**. It is an **act**. But it is also **presence of mind**. Hegel seems to hold out the vision, even the experience, of thinking as self-**presence**. Of being present to, or with, oneself — of being fully self-possessed, self-aware. Of self-consciousness as a huge, cosmic accomplishment.

Reading Hegel gives one a sense that the movement of thought will coincide with a vision of harmony that awaits us at the end of the whole process. Every serious reader of Hegel can bear witness to the intoxication of such moments.

Absolute Knowledge, in the form of the complete self-consciousness and self-possession of spirit, is only available at the end-point of the thinking process. But there is no distinction possible between the driving energy of thought and this sense of the harmony and fulfilment in the whole. It is ultimately the universal which has the upper hand. As Hegel's *Logic* puts it...

Everything depends on the "**identity** of identity and non-identity".

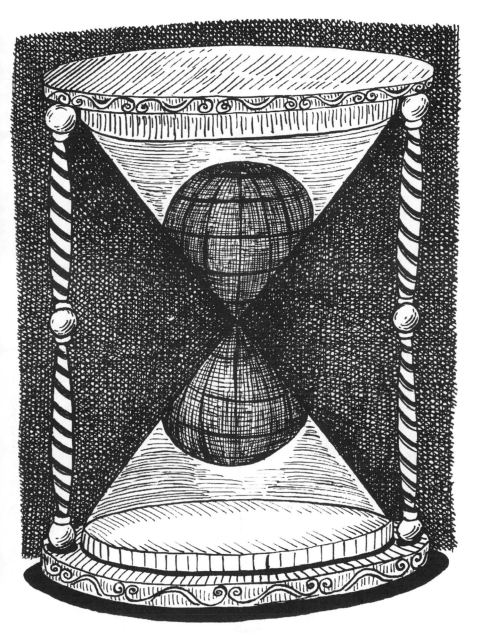

"In philosophy, the latest birth of time is the result of all the systems that have preceded it, and must include their principles; and so, if, on other grounds, it deserves the title of philosophy, it will be the fullest, most comprehensive, and most adequate system of all." Hegel, *Introduction to the Encyclopedia: Logic*

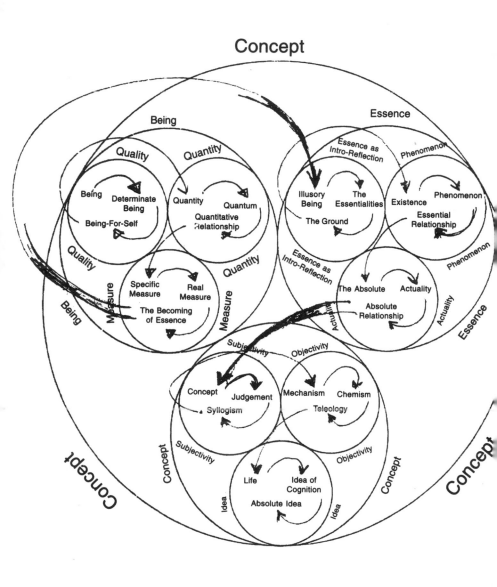

Concept

Essence

Being

Quality · Quantity

Essence as Intro-Reflection · Phenomenon

Being · Determinate Being
Being-For-Self

Quantity · Quantum
Quantitative Relationship

Illusory Being · The Essentialities
The Ground

Existence · Phenomenon
Essential Relationship

Quality

Quantity

Essence as Intro-Reflection

Phenomenon

Specific Measure · Real Measure
The Becoming of Essence

Measure

Measure

The Absolute · Actuality
Absolute Relationship

Actuality

Actuality

Essence

Being

Subjectivity · Objectivity

Concept · Judgement
Syllogism

Mechanism · Chemism
Teleology

Subjectivity

Objectivity

Concept

Concept

Life · Idea of Cognition
Absolute Idea

Idea

Idea

Concept

Concept

Concept

"Each of the parts of philosophy is a philosophical whole, a circle rounded and complete in itself... The whole of philosophy in this way resembles a circle of circles." Hegel, *Introduction to the Encyclopedia: Logic*

"The eternal life of God is to find himself, become aware of himself, coincide with himself. In this ascent there is an alienation, a disunion, but it is the nature of the spirit, of the Idea, to alienate itself in order to find itself again. This movement is just what freedom is; for, even looking at the matter from the outside, we say that the man is free who is not dependent on someone else, not oppressed, not involved with someone else. By reverting to itself, the spirit achieves its freedom — this universal movement is a series of the formations of the spirit. This series is not to be envisaged as a straight line, but as a circle returning into itself. This circle has for its circumference a great number of circles... In development [*Bildung*] there is an advance, not into the abstract infinite, but returning back into itself."

Success at Last!

The publication of the *Science of Logic* brought Hegel instant recognition. He received no less than three separate offers of a chair in philosophy, from Berlin, Heidelberg and Erlangen. Officials in Berlin expressed some doubts about Hegel's ability to teach his philosophy and make it comprehensible.

In 1816, Friedrich von Raumer, Professor of History in Breslau, was asked by the Minister for Trade, Culture and Education in Berlin to report on his visit to Hegel.

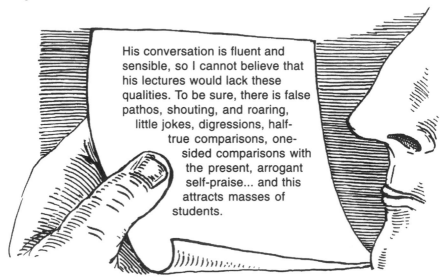

His conversation is fluent and sensible, so I cannot believe that his lectures would lack these qualities. To be sure, there is false pathos, shouting, and roaring, little jokes, digressions, half-true comparisons, one-sided comparisons with the present, arrogant self-praise... and this attracts masses of students.

Because of the uncertainty, there was some delay in actually sending off the offer from Berlin. On 30 July 1816, Hegel was offered a post at Heidelberg.

The Minister in Berlin asks me to judge for myself if I have "the ability to give vivid and incisive lectures"... Too late, I've already accepted the professorship in Heidelberg.

At the age of 46, Hegel went to Heidelberg to take up his first secure full-time academic post.

Professors were expected to base their lectures on *compendia*, short summaries of the great philosophical works of the past. A decade earlier — as *Privatdozent* in Jena — Hegel had spoken of presenting his students with a **system** of philosophy in the form of an *encyclopaedia*. Now, in order to make his own philosophy the basis of his lectures, Hegel dashed off his own highly abbreviated summary of his system.

Because the curriculum I devised as a schoolteacher contained practically my whole system, if only in skeletal form, I was able to provide a coherently systematic version in double-quick time.

It was published in 1817 as the ***Encyclopaedia of the Philosophical Sciences in Outline***. Hegel's philosophy had finally acquired its much-advertised systematic form.

This *Encyclopaedia* is the only complete and authentic statement of Hegel's philosophical system. But, as the title page bears out, it is **only an outline** intended for the guidance of struggling students. Instead of the free flight of speculation, we have the stumbling progress of the classroom. Paragraphs which are short and pregnant with meaning presuppose the presiding spirit of Hegel, as lecturer, to fuse them into a flowing discourse.

Hegel's *Encyclopaedia* is subdivided into three parts.

I. *Logic*

The *Encyclopaedia **Logic***, often termed the "lesser logic", is a distillation of Hegel's monumental *Science of Logic*, or "larger logic". These days the *Encyclopaedia* version is usually read in preference to the more elaborate, earlier version.

II. The *Philosophy of Nature*

The ***Philosophy of Nature*** stands on its own in Hegel's writings. It draws on Hegel's considerable knowledge of developments in the science of his day, but treats scientific principles in a uniquely Hegelian way.

III. The *Philosophy of Mind* (or *Spirit*, in German, *Geist*)

The third part of the *Encyclopaedia*, the ***Philosophy of Mind*** (or ***Spirit***) treats of everything specifically human.

The *Philosophy of Mind* is divided into three parts: ***Subjective Mind***, ***Objective Mind*** and ***Absolute Mind***.

Subjective Mind begins with sections on the physical, embodied individual and goes on to treat that individual under such headings as feelings and habit, perception, intellect and appetite. Then it treats of self-consciousness and reason and goes on to deal with the theoretical mind (including intuition, imagination and memory) and the practical mind.

Objective Mind treats of law, morality as well as social ethics. The section entitled "The Moral Life, or Social Ethics" is itself divided into three: it treats of the family, of civil society and the state. An expanded treatment of this material is given in the *Philosophy of Right*.

Absolute Mind is likewise divided in three: it treats of art, religion and philosophy.

The Reformers Call Hegel to Berlin

In the autumn of 1817 a new Prussian ministry for religious, educational and medical affairs was formed. Its first incumbent was Baron Karl Sigmund von Altenstein, one of Prussia's most progressive reformers and a long-time ally of the reforming State Chancellor Prince Karl August von Hardenberg. Within two months of taking office, von Altenstein wrote to Hegel.

Von Hardenberg

von Altenstein

Ah, he makes me another offer of a professorship in Berlin... and this time I accept!

Schleiermacher

Throughout his Berlin years Hegel enjoyed the support of von Altenstein. The Prussian state to which Hegel gave such devoted allegiance was the reformed and reforming Prussia of von Altenstein and von Hardenberg. But the opposition of the Romantic theologian, Friedrich Schleiermacher, prevented von Altenstein from having Hegel elected to the Royal Academy of Sciences as he had promised.

Hegel's Public Role in Berlin

In 1821, Hegel was appointed by von Altenstein to the Royal Academic Board of Examiners for the province of Brandenberg. Hegel was active in trying to promote the sort of humanistic education pioneered in Bavaria by his friend, Niethammer.

The social order Hegel defends from 1815 onwards is not the **old** order he had attacked so radically in 1801.

My views hadn't changed in the crucial decade between 1805 and 1815, but the whole fabric of German social and political life had been transformed under the tremendous jolt received from the Napoleonic wars. The system I appeared to defend after 1815 is precisely the one I wished to see established in 1802!

The Fall of Napoleon

All through the last years of Napoleon's rule, Hegel stood by his support of the French. The subjective Romanticism of the 1813 German national uprising in resistance to the French ran contrary to all of Hegel's conceptions about the nature of politics. In fact, Hegel opposed the first expressions of violent German nationalism in this resistance.

Napoleon's defeat and abdication came as a great shock to Hegel.

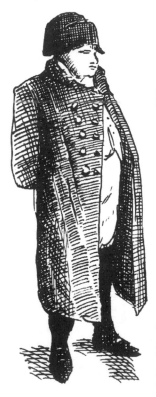

It is an immense spectacle to see an enormous genius destroy himself. This is the most tragic thing that exists.

When Napoleon returned from Elba, Hegel entertained no hope for a comeback. He knew that all was lost. Yet, he confides in a letter, if he had harboured any hopes for a possible Napoleonic victory, he would have "put a rifle on his shoulder" and gone to join him.

Hegel's Politics

Hegel's political development has frequently been misinterpreted. It is worth looking at in some detail.

Hegel started out a radical, wanting to use a new and revitalized religion to overcome crises of public and political life.

The dream, which I shared with Hölderlin, of becoming a kind of secular priest, teaching the philosophy of spirit, rather than conventional pieties, was one I had to carry through on my own.

von Hardenberg

von Altenstein

When he finally received the call to Berlin in 1818, it was from two men — von Altenstein and von Hardenberg — who had played a prominent and progressive role in Prussia's "peaceful revolution from above" for over a decade.

The Rise of a New Right

By the time Hegel arrived in Berlin, the momentum for reform had diminished. A "new right" among the Prussian Junker class was seeking to reinstitute feudal privileges enjoyed before Napoleonic times. They had allies among intellectuals and academics.

Many who started out as Romantics and revolutionaries were now espousing reaction and chauvinistic nationalism.

And there was a new mood afoot among the students with the rise in 1816 of the *Burschenschaften* student movement.

Young men returned from the Napoleonic wars changed the nature of student politics in Germany. They expected promises of constitutional change in the liberated German states to be honoured, but also introduced a new note of extreme nationalism.

Nationalism and Anti-Semitism

In the Preface to the *Philosophy of Right*, Hegel attacked his erstwhile colleague, **Jacob Friedrich Fries** (1773-1843), "commander-in-chief of prevalent shallowness" and a "pettifogging advocate of arbitrariness".

Fries had been barred from giving public lectures after taking part in the mass demonstrations at Wartburg organized in 1817 by the *Burschenschaften* to protest against the policies of the German Confederation.

We burned a large pile of books by authors we objected to.

In his pamphlet, ***On the Danger Posed to the Welfare and Character of the German People by the Jews***, Fries attacked the Jewish "bloodsuckers" and advocated the suppression of Jewish educational institutions.

Fries's violently anti-Semitic programme reads like a draft of the Nazi Nuremberg race laws. He began as a post-Kantian logician and ended an advocate of racist chauvinism and even terrorism.

Against Moral Subjectivism

In 1819, a student of theology, Karl Ludwig Sand, murdered the reactionary Russophile poet, August Friedrich Kotzebue (whom the students suspected of being a Russian agent).

The Berlin theologian, Wilhelm Martin de Wette, a follower of Fries's philosophy of immediate feeling, wrote a letter of consolation to Sand's mother in which he talked of the "pure intentions" of the assassin. In the *Philosophy of Right*, Hegel argued that such moral subjectivism can be used to justify any crime.

This moral subjectivism leads to an aversion to any objective or codified system of law, and to moral relativism.

In 1819, the anti-Semitism of the *Burschenschaften* erupted in street violence in Frankfurt. The actions and ideology of these extremists prefigure the ultra-nationalist fascism that would emerge almost a hundred years later in Germany.

Hegel's Lectures

From this point on, in accordance with his new status and public role in Berlin, Hegel's philosophizing takes the form of lectures. He was to publish only one more textbook, the *Philosophy of Right*. We shall be looking at the following main lectures.

Lectures on the Philosophy of World History

Lectures on Aesthetics (or the Philosophy of Art)

Lectures on the Philosophy of Religion

Lectures on the History of Philosophy

Freedom and the State

The two concepts **freedom** and the **state** are at the heart of Hegel's whole treatment of politics, ethics and history. There are no two concepts more controversial or more complex in all his work.

What do you mean by "freedom"?

I certainly don't mean "licence". Only as a social being who partakes in ethical life is the individual truly a person.

According to Hegel, the will is essentially free. This distinguishes us from the animals: having purposes and striving deliberately to achieve them. To possess a will means wanting to be free and therefore, to some extent, already being so. But only abstractly. The realization (*Verwirklichung*) of freedom — its becoming actual (*Wirklichkeit*) — is as much social as personal.

The State

What we normally mean by the "state" is a set of institutions (police, judiciary, army, education, etc.) which governs life in any modern nation.

I don't mean a set of institutions but the objective embodiment of **ethical life**.

Hegel's political vision derives from the ancient Greeks. His theory of the modern state aims to recapture the Greeks' quasi-religious sense of commitment to community (the *polis*). His argument is neither nostalgic nor conservative, as we will see.

The Evolution of Freedom

Hegel acknowledges that slavery was integral to the social fabric of Greek democracy.

The Greeks knew only that some men are free. To Christianity we owe the insight that all men **should** be free. But it takes the entire Christian epoch to arrive at the point where freedom for all humanity becomes practically possible.

Freedom has to take shape in the individual consciousness and will. But having been developed in the form of the **individualization** of the modern age, it must still develop its social side. At first it does so abstractly, in the opposition between duty and individual inclination (in systems of ethics culminating in that of Kant). Only as a final result does freedom become aware of itself as having a history and a social dimension.

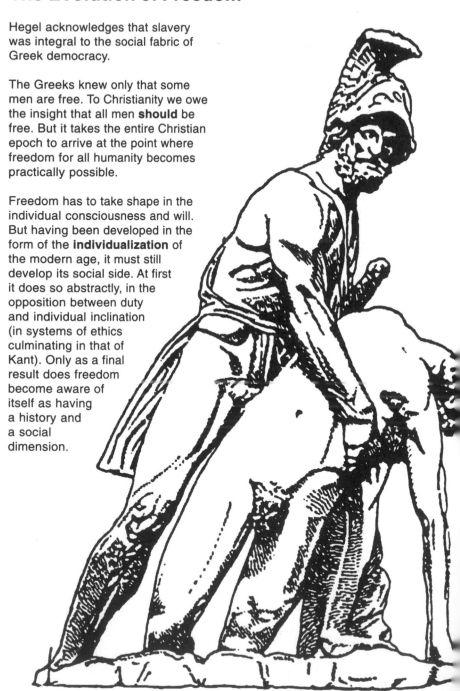

The *Philosophy of Right*

Let's begin by considering Hegel's view of modern individualism, not abstractly but as expressed in the social arrangements themselves. For instance, Part One of the *Philosophy of Right* (1821) deals with the **laws of property**.

Property is not something natural — as it is for John Locke — but founded on **convention**.

"Private" property is a social or public relation which depends on recognition by others. While **possession** relates to the individual, **property** relates the individual to society.

Social Ethics

Part Two, on **Morality**, relates the rights of moral subjects to the responsibility for one's actions. Part Three, on **Social Ethics**, involves three interrelated domains: the **family**, **civil society** and the **state**.

The family not only perpetuates the human organism (through reproduction) but also raises human beings.

Its socialization of the individual transforms biological and psychological needs into individual desires.

Because the vast majority of families do not produce their own subsistence, they must have dealings with other families in the economic and civil life of society.

Civil Society

Civil society involves the production, distribution and consumption of products to meet the variety of needs and wants.

This system of needs answers natural impulses and needs, but at the same time modifies and multiplies those needs.

Civil society has its own institutions (the Administration of Justice, Public Authority, Corporations) to regulate and facilitate activities. Hegel calls these institutions of civil society the "external state" because they are treated as mere instruments for achieving personal aims.

Karl Marx (1818-83) acknowledged the importance of these passages in Hegel's *Philosophy of Right*.

The state outlined by Hegel is less like the actual Prussian state of his day than like the plans for a new constitution drafted by Chancellor von Hardenberg in 1819, but never implemented. Hegel, like von Hardenberg, endorses constitutional monarchy.

The state is no work of art; it stands on earth and so in the sphere of caprice, chance and error. For any state, world history represents the last judgement.

Hegel clearly wished to believe that Prussia, the home of German intellectual life, could and would be a state "ethical of purpose". Although born a Swabian, he became a Prussian patriot by conviction, but he was never a German nationalist. He was not guilty of any form of chauvinism and remained throughout his life opposed to every form of conservatism. He was only driven to defend the status quo against the rise of the New Right.

"The Actual is the Rational"

Hegel insisted that it was no part of philosophy's role to instruct rulers or anyone else on what "ought to be". Its role was limited to showing what was reasonable in each particular case. Philosophy had to show that...

> What is rational is actual, and what is actual is rational.

Generations of commentators have castigated Hegel for this formula. But the nature of Hegel's "system" means no other idea is feasible. Hegel's philosophy is retrospective through and through. Every aspect of it is historical — but all of history is taken up (and thus "cancelled") in the system. **Genesis becomes structure.**

Throughout the last decade of his life. Hegel wrestled with insoluble conundrums created by the inexorability of his own logic. His system is a closed one. He had the job of expounding and elaborating it. But his mind, and his life, were not closed. His system resolves all of history into an eternal image. But he still had to live, and he knew himself to be as much subject to history and its vagaries as anyone else.

Although outwardly happy and successful. Hegel admitted that he was never able to free himself of "anxieties and doubts".

The Philosophy of History

Hegel claims to show that history itself — with all its accidents and unforeseeable events — obeys a certain logic and could be said to reveal an idea. For Hegel, that idea is **Freedom**.

Hegel delivered his lectures on the Philosophy of History in the years 1822-3 and 1830-1. The introduction explains the principle which guides his study: the unfolding of the spirit, and of freedom, in stages. Spirit is opposed to (the contrary of) nature.

So progress in the unfolding of spirit toward freedom is progress in liberation from subjection to nature.

THE PHILOSOPHY OF HISTORY

The Course of World History

World History (or Universal History) consists of the transactions of world-historical peoples who play their parts successively on the historical scene.

It begins with the **Oriental World** (China, India and Persia).

Then it goes on to develop a contrast between the civilizations of the ancient Greeks and the Romans.

The "Germanic World"

Hegel's next stage is the **"Germanic World"** which covers all of Western Europe from the birth of Christianity to the present.

I refer to the Germanic World, because the Protestant countries of northern Europe are closer to realizing the European ideal than the Romance peoples of Catholic Europe.

Under the heading of the "Germanic World", Hegel traces the path of European history from feudalism and the age of the Church up to the Reformation, and then on to the Enlightenment and the French Revolution.

The world history of "freedom" is treated in three simple stages.

Stage One — the ancient Orient — only one (the ruler) is free.
Stage Two — classical Antiquity — some (but not slaves) are free.
Stage Three — the Christian-Germanic epoch — begins with the realization that all should be free, or, as Hegel puts it, that "man as man is free".

Via a long process, history arrives at the French Revolution when freedom becomes a practical proposition..

The Orient knew and knows only that **one** man is free, the Greek and Roman world that **some** are free, the Germanic world knows that **all** are free.

117

Freedom Without a Future?

So much of Hegel's philosophy is about "freedom" that it is worth considering some of the difficulties that his dialectical concept contains.

For us moderns, "freedom" is usually associated with an open field of possibilities and unpredictability. "Freedom" implies a **future** without any foregone conclusions.

But my philosophical system does not envisage the future.

Like the "contingency" of nature, "the future" remains a mere category — defined simply as something inaccessible to the form-giving (or form-revealing) activity of philosophical reflection. "The past is preserved by the present, as reality, but the future is the opposite of this, or rather it is the formless... no form whatsoever can be discerned in the future."

"If the forests of Germania had still existed, there would have been no French Revolution... America is thus the land of the future in which, in times to come, possibly in a fight between North and South America, some world-historical significance is to be revealed... It is not the philosopher's business to prophesy. As far as history goes, we must rather deal with what has been and with what is — in philosophy, on the other hand, with what neither merely has been nor merely will be, but with what **is** and is eternally: with Reason, and with that we have enough to do."

The Philosophy of Nature

In the opening words of the *Philosophy of Nature* (1817) Hegel confronts the fact that the very idea of a **philosophy** of nature was no longer fashionable. It is even less fashionable today. With the result that Hegel's "philosophy of nature" is often passed over in embarrassment, even by his most enthusiastic commentators.

At the end of the 18th and the beginning of the 19th centuries, there had been a great deal of philosophizing about nature.

Electricity was a new and awesome discovery and was seen by many as having cosmic significance. Schelling's own "philosophy of nature" made a good deal of the opposition between positive and negative poles.

Unsatisfactory Science

Hegel acknowledges that the natural sciences were already progressing without help from philosophy. He does not wish to confuse the imperatives of philosophy with "scientific procedure". It is exactly "such charlatanism" — "especially Schelling's" — which had led to the Philosophy of Nature being discredited.

What is Nature?... Nature confronts us as a riddle and a problem, whose solution both attracts and repels us: attracts us because Spirit is presaged in Nature; repels us because Nature seems an alien existence, in which Spirit does not find itself. That is why Aristotle said that philosophy started from wonder.

The properly scientific approach, which starts with the collection of facts and looks for the laws of nature, "runs on into endless detail in all directions, and just because no end can be perceived in it, this method does not satisfy us".

Science is Incomplete Understanding

Science may increase our understanding of the variety and the ways of nature. But Hegel demands an **Idea** of Nature. Nature must fit into the scheme of things as revealed by Reason.

Hegel accepted and developed Kant's distinction that the understanding, although a necessary stage of thought, is less philosophical than Reason.

To think in terms of the understanding, as is done in mathematics, the natural sciences and traditional metaphysics, is to think in terms of fixed or uncriticized categories, to think undialectically or in pre-philosophical terms.

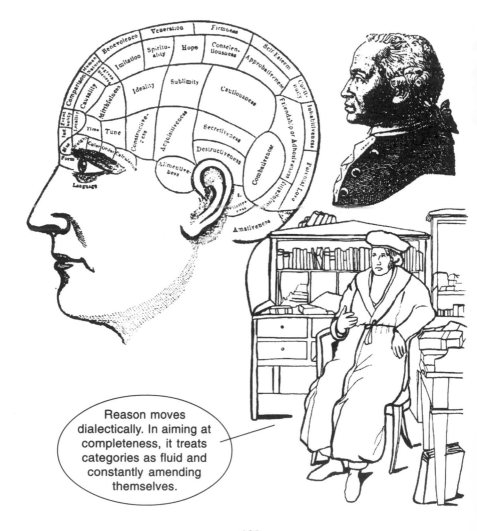

Reason moves dialectically. In aiming at completeness, it treats categories as fluid and constantly amending themselves.

Nature as Idea

But a Philosophy of Nature is an essential part of Hegel's whole system. As an Idea, Nature forms part of Hegel's version of the Fall and the (slow, logical process of) Ascension. If the Logic is the Idea in itself, before the Fall, then Nature is the "**self-degradation of the Idea**" which has become external to itself. Hegel explains the role of Nature in theological terms and even refers to the German mystic, Jakob Boehme.

Nature has no history and shows no development. Its rigid and timeless laws must be obeyed, but remain external to subjectivity. But Hegel must show how freedom, and therefore history, is possible.

This transition from necessity to freedom is not a simple transition but a progression through many stages, whose exposition constitutes the Philosophy of Nature.

The Philosophy of Art

Hegel's *Lectures on Aesthetics* encompass the whole history of art and its central role in the development of human culture. Art, religion and philosophy are humanity's supreme attainments or (what amounts to the same thing) aspects of the self-revelation of God or the "Absolute".

Hegel's account of beauty is a modification of Schiller's view in *Letters on the Aesthetic Education of Mankind* (1795).

Beauty is the mediation between the sensible (or sensuous) and the rational (or intellectual). My definition of beauty as "pure appearance of the Idea to sense" is true of beauty throughout the history of its embodiment in art.

For Hegel, beauty in art reveals absolute truth, but does so through **feeling** and **perception**. The best art reveals what is unconditionally true.

Art in Relation to Religion and Philosophy

Hegel treats art as being capable of conveying the deepest metaphysical or philosophical insights and as intimately linked to both religion and philosophy itself. The medium of art is **sensation**, the medium of religion is **mental imagery** (or internal pictures of "what is godlike"). The realm of philosophy is pure **imageless conception**. This parallels the progression in Plato towards pure apprehension of Ideas.

Art and religion are intimately linked because both are grounded in sensation.

Both depend on "picture-thinking" in their attempts to apprehend the divine.

But art has the particular task of showing, within the realm of the human, the essence of the divine.

Symbolic, Classic and Romantic Art

This allows Hegel to link the histories of religion and art. Certain conceptions of the divine are better suited to artistic expression than others, which leads to Hegel's classification of art into **Symbolic**, **Classic** and **Romantic**.

Early nature religions saw the divine not in human form, but either in natural forces or life in general.

Their conceptions of the divine were too vague and indeterminate to be sensuously embodied in fine art.

The art engendered by such religions is described as being "Symbolic" (it uses animal symbols and the like), which grasps its subject matter (the divine) only indirectly or approximately.

Classic or Greek Art

Greek (Classical) art takes the human as measure of the divine. This is the heart of Hegel's treatment of art. Greek or Classical sculpture achieves the epitome of artistic beauty because it embraces the **whole** human being.

The histories of civilization, religion and philosophy improve and progress as they advance from their beginnings in the East and reach their peak in modern (that is to say, Hegel's) times. By contrast, art reaches its peak in Greece. The modern period is treated as a period of artistic decline.

Only in Greek art do message (or content) and medium (or form) coincide. In Greek sculpture, Hegel sees the essential message of art adequately expressed in concrete, sensuous form.

Romantic Art

Hegel treats all art from the Greeks onwards as "Romantic", which includes the art of the Christian medieval period (and, indeed, begins even earlier with Roman stoicism). It is more personal, inward, ideally non-empirical. The conception of what is human is concentrated into the intangible, alien to the physical body. It is idealized as the immortal soul (or inner character). This drives art of the Romantic phase to reach deeper into human subjectivity.

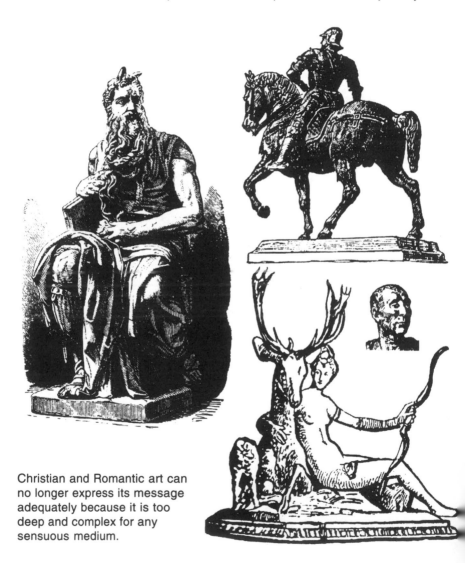

Christian and Romantic art can no longer express its message adequately because it is too deep and complex for any sensuous medium.

The Five Arts

Hegel accepts the conventional five-fold classification of the arts: architecture, sculpture, painting, music and poetry. Each particular artistic discipline is seen as having been characteristic or dominant at a particular point in the history of art. Architecture was dominant for Symbolic art, sculpture during the Classical period. Painting, music and poetry are stages of the modern or Romantic period.

Art begins with the triumph of mind over matter.

Architecture sees its task as to work inorganic nature into a shape that becomes allied to the mind, an artistically valid "outside world".

The Ideal in Painting

The beauty of an artwork corresponds to its degree of organization or integration. No elements of an artwork may appear arbitrary, unplanned, accidental or irrational. Hegel sometimes attributes perfection to an artwork as a consequence of its idealization of a given subject matter. "... [The artist] must omit little hairs, pores, little scars, blemishes, and grasp and represent the subject in its universal character and in its steadfast individuality. It makes a great difference whether the artist merely reproduces a person's physiognomy, as it quietly presents itself to him in its surface and external configuration, or whether the artist insightfully represents the true features which express the subject's own soul."

For the Ideal necessitates, without exception, that the external form accord with the soul.

Poetry, the Highest Art

Poetry is seen as the most profound art because it enjoys the most detached relation between its medium (language) and any idea or content. Hegel bases this judgement on the arbitrary or merely conventional relation between verbal sounds and their meaning. Dog, *Hund*, *chien*, *cane*, *perro* all represent the same thought. One word can be substituted for another in translation. Thus language shows itself to be merely a vehicle and not constitutive of thought.

The verbal form of poetry serves merely as a transparent skin through which we apprehend its distinctly thoughtful nature.

As we progress from architecture to sculpture, painting, music and poetry, the sensuous medium becomes less and less conspicuous — until in poetry it becomes a mere inessential convention. Poetry strives to become philosophy.

Philosophy, Higher than Art

Philosophy is on a higher plane than art or religion, which are still tied to "picture-thinking".

We recall that the first two divisions of Hegel's *Logic* ("Being" and "Essence") are still tied to "representation" (*Vorstellung*) or **image**-ination, whereas in the final division (the "Notion"), we enter the realms of pure thought or the wholly conceptual. Truth proper is, according to Hegel, "imageless".

So, religion and art are destined to be superseded by philosophy which is able to dispense with the sensuous and to deal in purely conceptual terms.

Art in its later phases points beyond itself towards higher, more philosophic forms of cultural expression.

In medieval times, religion and philosophy became independent of art. The inner depths of the Christian God and of Christian man elude full expression in art. Art loses the internal harmony which it displayed in Classical times, because it points to a meaning which art itself cannot fully express. It becomes **allegory**.

Art turns increasingly abstract and poses the problem of self-reflexive irony.

The Problem of Irony

During this whole Christian Romantic period, abstract reflective thought invades art and it becomes less sensuous and more conceptual. Hegel decries this development because it means a detachment from any firm, definite vision. Art succumbs to **irony** and gives itself over to unending reflection: reflection on societies, philosophies, religions and types of art; reflections on the criteria for assessing them; reflection on the criteria for assessing those criteria.

The isolated ego, detached from its own time and place, can range freely in imagination — and in allegiance — over other times and places.

The ironist is adept at reconciling apparently incompatible points of view — which sounds remarkably like Hegel's own procedure.

In Hegel's own day, the early German Romantics, **Friedrich Schlegel** (1772-1829) and **Novalis** (1772-1801), had developed a philosophy of art centred on the concept of **Romantic Irony**. Drawing inspiration mainly from Fichte, they praised the reflexive nature of art works.

Great art is able to comment on itself.

The reflexive, or open, work of art can assimilate a range of artistic impulses and forms and comment on them all.

Romantic irony already points to the familiar tricks of 20th century "postmodern" art — self-conscious pastiche, parody and relativism.

The End of Art

In the process of its development, history empties itself into system. Systematic impulses end up elaborating themselves in a complex logical structure. **Process becomes product**. It is in this sense that we must understand Hegel's talk of "an end of art".

It seems that art has exhausted all its significant possibilities. There is nothing left for it to do but produce new variations on old themes.

150 years later, Hegel's verdict is confirmed by the artists and theorists of postmodernism who confess that theirs is an "art of exhaustion".

This means that the problem of reflective irony can be solved **for** philosophy **within** philosophy.

This is Hegel's justification for providing us with a "philosophy of art". The Philosophy of Art performs a task which is beyond the capacity of art itself — that of surveying the diversity of art forms and of integrating them into a single coherent system.

But "system" also implies completeness and an "end". Postmodernism acknowledges that art is in a strange condition of "after-life", a predicament foreseen by Hegel's logic of history. Marx, and in our own day, Fukuyama, have been tempted by the possibility that history itself might have an "end" (purpose and finality).

The Philosophy of Religion

Hegel's thinking on religion evolved from his student dreams of a new *Volksreligion*. Religion keeps its important place in his mature philosophy as a way of apprehending and expressing the Absolute.

Religion transcends Art because it actually **thinks** the Absolute, whereas Art merely expresses it in figurative form.

But Hegel is clear: philosophy goes beyond both art and religion because it expresses the Absolute in pure speculative terms and is therefore able to synthesize all other forms of expression.

The Trinity

Nevertheless, Hegel often employs religious imagery in his major works, especially the image of the Christian Trinity to illustrate the pattern of the Idea and Absolute Spirit. Christian theology "pictures" God as a Trinity, and conceives of his life as a **triadic process**, very like Hegel's own process of dialectical sublation.

God (Truth) posits the Other: he begets and recognizes himself in the Son, a relationship which is mediated by the Holy Spirit.

Mystic Diagrams

Hegel had borrowed the diagram from the occult writings of his contemporary, **Franz von Baader** (1765-1841), who attempted to give geometrical expression to the mystical ideas of Jakob Boehme, the 17th century shoemaker of Görlitz. When you move the three smaller triangles into the big one you get...

Hegel experimented with such diagrams, but they proved too static. His philosophy is a dynamic one which requires the idea of "imageless truth".

Hegel's thinking can be seen as a form of mysticism — a mysticism of Reason. Hegel acknowledged the inspiration of the mystics.

"Speculative truth means very much the same as what, in special connection with religious experience and doctrines, used to be called Mysticism."

But Hegel's mysticism was emphatically a mysticism without mystery. Whereas most mystics end in silence, Hegel is determined to say everything! He accepts the mystical first words of St John's Gospel, "In the Beginning was the Word (*Logos*)", but interprets *Logos* as the "Idea in-itself".

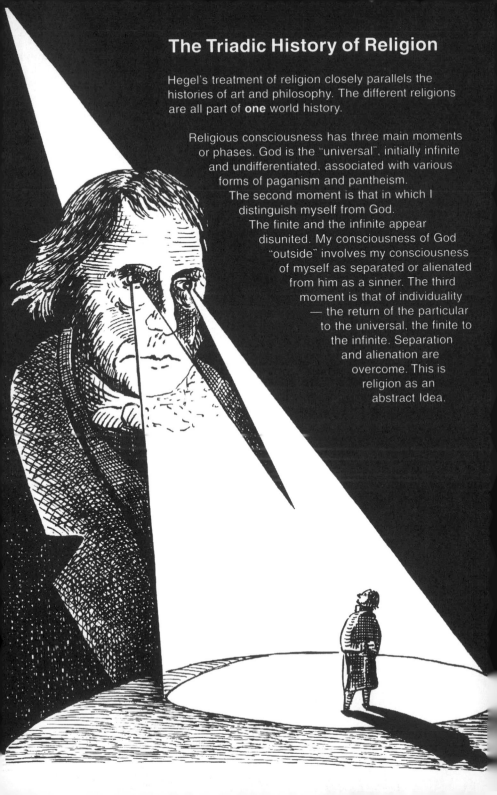

The Triadic History of Religion

Hegel's treatment of religion closely parallels the histories of art and philosophy. The different religions are all part of **one** world history.

Religious consciousness has three main moments or phases. God is the "universal", initially infinite and undifferentiated, associated with various forms of paganism and pantheism. The second moment is that in which I distinguish myself from God. The finite and the infinite appear disunited. My consciousness of God "outside" involves my consciousness of myself as separated or alienated from him as a sinner. The third moment is that of individuality — the return of the particular to the universal, the finite to the infinite. Separation and alienation are overcome. This is religion as an abstract Idea.

The Politics of Religion

Between 1821 and 1831, Hegel gave four series of lectures on religion. They were intended to be controversial and to challenge the Romantic theologian **Friedrich Schleiermacher** (1768-1834).

The essence of religion is **the feeling of absolute dependence**. I repudiated rational thought in favour of a theology of feeling.

— Schleiermacher

If religion in a human being is founded only on a feeling, the latter has no other function than to be the feeling of his dependency, and thus a dog would be the best Christian... A dog even has feelings of "salvation", when its hunger is satisfied by a bone.

— Hegel in a preface to **On Religion in an Inner Relationship to Science** (1822) by **H.F.W. Hinrichs** (1794-1861), probably the first to teach the Hegelian system.

By 1821, a reactionary religio-political coalition of Protestants was forming around the figure of the Crown Prince, the future Frederick Wilhelm IV of Prussia, who had come under the influence of the Rosicrucians, an occult, cabbalistic sect.

Hegel admitted to his friend Niethammer that his influence was confined to academic circles and the development of a "school of thought".

As a professor, I have only begun. Much still remains to be achieved for me and the Cause.

Embarrassed and angered by the tendency of German thinkers to organize philosophy around feeling and fantasy, Hegel offered speculative philosophy as a method for teaching students how to think.

In 1821, a royal edict instructed von Altenstein, the Minister for Culture and Education, to prohibit the teaching of "speculative philosophy" (meaning Hegel's ideas) at the University of Berlin. Altenstein refused. A series of spokesmen for neo-pietistic conservatives continued to accuse Hegel of "**panlogicism**".

Panlogicism — or in other words — **atheism**!

I have explained and expressed Luther's teaching as true and as recognized by philosophy as true.

Hegel sincerely believed in his legitimate development of the Lutheran programme. Whereas the Catholic idea of ecclesiastical authority would have been incompatible with Hegel's philosophy, Luther's establishment of "inner freedom" was in accord with it.

The English Reform Bill of 1830

Hegel's last published writing was a long essay on the English Reform Bill which appeared in the official *Preussische Staatszeitung* (Prussian Government Newspaper) in 1831. The last instalment was suppressed by Prussian censorship and only circulated privately. Hegel casts doubt on the Reform Bill, but his argument is far from a defence of the status quo. He is scathing about social conditions in England.

Hegel saw that mere reform of the voting system would not cure England's social problems.

The whole of English law rests on "the English principle of **positivity**" — its provisions legitimized only by precedent and continuity. To this English principle, the Reform Bill "administers a shock" as the first real attempt to make the political and legal system of England conform to Reason. But behind the inadequacies of the Bill, Hegel sees the self-interest of the new middle-class which has made reform serve its own coming to power.

The End

Hegel's last years were deeply troubled ones. In July 1830 there was a *coup d'état* in Paris itself. Unrest (which Hegel referred to as "the carnival") spread quickly to Belgium, Poland and the very borders of Prussia. Only in the latter part of his life had Europe been free from war. Now, he confided, "It is a crisis in which everything that was formerly valid appears to be made problematic".

Nearing the end of what turned out to be his last lecture on world history, he resigned himself to the thought that...

"This collision, this nodus, this problem is one whose solution history has to work out in the future."

Hegel became ill and died quietly on 13 November 1831. He was buried, as he had requested, next to Fichte.

The Decline of Hegelianism

Within a few years of Hegel's arrival in Berlin, his students and followers had become an organized academic school of thought. They created a Society of Scientific Criticism and published their own academic journal (for which they managed to receive a state subsidy).

Away from Berlin, Hegelianism was a minority perspective, even among academics. Neo-Kantianism and the influence of Romanticism in philosophy, theology and jurisprudence held sway in other universities.

After Hegel's death, the influence of his philosophy waned still further. But it kept a few fiercely loyal adherents.

Hegelians Left, Right and Centre

Hegel's followers, the "Young Hegelians", soon split into "right", "left" and "centre" over questions of theology.

"Right" Hegelians defended **traditional** Christianity, at the same time assimilating what bits of the system they could.

"Centre" Hegelians sought to reinterpret religious dogma in Hegelian terms to give it a new, more scientific language.

"Left" Hegelians criticized Christianity and developed Hegel's ideas towards radical (even atheistic) conclusions.

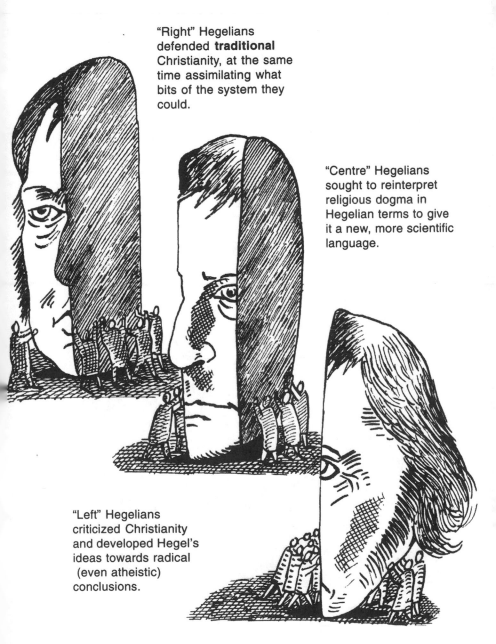

The Left or Young Hegelians

The Left Hegelians tended to be more radical not only in theology, but also on social and political questions. **Moses Hess** (1812-75) explicitly linked Hegelian ideas to the support of the Communist workers' movement in *The European Triarchy* (1841).

In the period 1843-6, all of the major theorists and journalistic publicists of the Left Hegelian movement engaged in divisive criticism of one another, each one accusing his former comrades of remaining caught in the "theological" illusions of a language of "essence".

Feuerbach's *Essence of Christianity*

Another important Left Hegelian, **Ludwig Feuerbach** (1804-72) wanted to turn Hegel's theory into practice. As early as 1828, he wrote to Hegel about his efforts to "actualize and secularize the Idea".

Christianity prevents humanity from realizing itself in the Absolute. A new age is dawning in which Christian values will be abolished from human consciousness and man will conceive of himself as a natural being.

Twaddle! I am a Lutheran and detest seeing Lutheranism explained in the same manner as the descent and dissemination of silk culture, cherries, smallpox and the like.

Feuerbach's *Essence of Christianity* (1841) attempted to go beyond Hegel's metaphysics and enshrine **humankind** in place of his Absolute Spirit.

LUDWIG FEUERBACH

The German Ideology

Left Hegelians shared an agenda of comprehending reality as finite existence and Reason as a product of human actions. Their aim was a final liberation from the illusions of Christian culture, as well as from Hegel's translation of that culture into the metaphysics of his system.

In 1845-6, Marx and Engels collaborated on writing *The German Ideology*.

Here we began to develop our view of history later called **"historical materialism"**.

We satirized the Young Hegelians and their simple "inversion" of Hegel.

Marx also wrote his *Theses on Feuerbach* in 1845, ending with the famous words: "The philosophers have only **interpreted** the world in various ways; the point is to **change** it."

I would greatly like to make accessible to the ordinary human intelligence, in two or three printer's sheets, what is **rational** in the method which Hegel discovered but at the same time enveloped in mysticism.

(Marx)

What distinguishes Hegel's mode of thinking from that of all other philosophers is the exceptional historical sense underlying it.

(Engels)

It is impossible completely to understand Marx's *Capital*, and especially its first chapter, without having thoroughly studied and understood the whole of Hegel's *Logic*. Consequently, half a century later, none of the Marxists has understood Marx!

(Lenin)

An End to Reason

Marx's insistence on the **rationality** of Hegel's method was uncharacteristic of the main later 19th century thinkers. The problem was, Hegel had succeeded in persuading even his critics that his system contained all previous standpoints as subsidiary components of itself. Hence, the question of Hegel became the question of the survival of philosophical rationality itself!

After Hegel's death, the rest of the 19th century belongs to those who questioned the role of philosophical reasoning itself and sought to replace it. **Positivism** and **Existentialism** were two such outcomes.

Auguste Comte (1798-1857) proclaimed the coming age of positive science (positivism) with its reliance on empirical evidence.

This will finally put an end to metaphysics.

I was the first to express the concept of existential anguish and the irrational leap of faith.

Søren Kierkegaard (1813-55) declared the bankruptcy of Reason.

The Origins of Existentialism

In 1841, Schelling was invited to Berlin. His task, according to the new Prussian Minister of Culture, was "to expunge the dragon's seed of Hegelian pantheism" from the minds of Prussian youth. In his first lecture, Schelling insisted that the task of refuting Hegel had already been accomplished by "life".

Schelling's own mystical ideas failed to win many converts and attendance at his lectures was disappointing.

But my criticism of Hegel struck a chord!

Schelling argued that Hegel's whole system was based on a confusion of "essence" and "existence". A return to the philosophy of **existence** was necessary.

Kierkegaard was in the audience. Others included the Russian anarchist **Mikhail Bakunin** (1814-76) and the young **Friedrich Engels** (1820-95).

Kierkegaard accused modern philosophy — meaning Hegel — of being based on a **comical** presupposition.

One that is occasioned by its having forgotten, in a sort of world-historical absentmindedness, what it means to be a human being.

Hegel's retrospective world history, bereft of a future, struck Kierkegaard as equally inhuman.

"It may be that life can only be understood backwards, but it has to be lived forwards."

NIETZSCHE

SARTRE

HUSSERL

Existentialism begins with Kierkegaard's sense of human absurdity. It later develops, via **F.W. Nietzsche**, psychoanalysis and the phenomenology of **Edmund Husserl**, into the different "existentialisms" of **Martin Heidegger** and **Jean-Paul Sartre**.

Is Hegel Still Important?

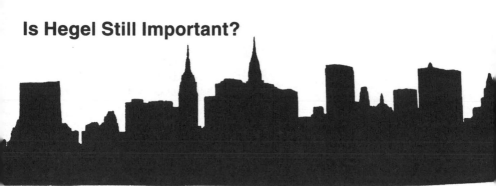

One could write an intellectual history of our century without mentioning Hegel. The 19th century thinkers whose spirits have dominated the 20th century have been Marx, Kierkegaard and Nietzsche. At the beginning of this century, **Sigmund Freud** brought to light the unconscious and **Ferdinand de Saussure** the structure of language. Meanwhile, science has made explosive progress, more or less oblivious to the continuing debates among philosophers of science.

It is possible to leave Hegel out of the picture.

FREUD

SAUSSURE

Possible, but not advisable.

Towards the Postmodern Impasse

Maurice Merleau-Ponty
(1908-61), a distinguished phenomenologist, has put the case for Hegel in our century.

All the great philosophical ideas of the past century — the philosophies of Marx and Nietzsche, phenomenology, German existentialism, and psychoanalysis — had their beginnings in Hegel... No task in the cultural order is more urgent than re-establishing the connection between, on the one hand, the thankless doctrines which try to forget their Hegelian origin and, on the other, that origin itself.

(Maurice Merleau-Ponty)

Hegel's importance is acknowledged even by those like **Jacques Derrida** (b. 1930) who wish to oppose or "deconstruct" his influence.

Hegelianism only extends its historical domination, finally unfolding its immense enveloping resources without obstacle.

(Jacques Derrida)

And in his inaugural address at the *Collège de France* (1970), **Michel Foucault** (1926-84) declared that...

Whether through logic or epistemology, whether through Marx or Nietzsche, our entire epoch struggles to disentangle itself from Hegel.

(Michel Foucault)

And the postmodern philosopher, **Richard Rorty** (b. 1931)...

Philosophers are doomed to find Hegel waiting patiently at the end of whatever road we travel.

(Richard Rorty)

Rediscovering Hegel and Marx

In 1906, **Wilhelm Dilthey** published a monograph on the young Hegel, and in 1907 **Hermann Nohl**'s edition of *Hegel's Early Theological Writings* appeared. A new, radical "unfinished" Hegelianism became discernible.

When Marx's early writings — in particular the 1844 *Economic and Philosophical Manuscripts* — were published in the 1920s, they revealed how much of Marx's own radical philosophy had been developed through his reading of Hegel.

Today we can see that the young Marx, who had no access to the writings of the young Hegel, retraced much of the same ground. The young Marx and the young Hegel are extraordinarily close in spirit.

In the early part of the 20th century, many Marxist intellectuals realized that Marx's schematic treatment of history needed re-examination. Their concerns were sharpened by the cataclysm of the 1914-18 war, the success of a Communist revolution in pre-capitalist Russia and the failure of similar revolutionary attempts in more developed countries such as Germany. **Gyorgy Lukaçs** (1885-1971), a Hungarian revolutionary intellectual, led the way.

Lukaçs's *History and Class Consciousness* influenced a whole generation of "Hegelian-Marxists" that included **Ernst Bloch**, **Herbert Marcuse**, **Theodor W. Adorno** and **Max Horkheimer**.

Adorno

Marcuse

LUKAÇS

Bloch

I renewed Marxist philosophy, reintegrating it with ideas more fully developed in Hegel.

These last three were influential protagonists of the **Frankfurt School** of Marxism (founded 1923).

161

Critical Theory

ADORNO

BENJAMIN

MARCUSE

The Frankfurt School members, **Adorno**, **Marcuse** and **Walter Benjamin**, were all deeply concerned with art, music and literature — the "aesthetic dimension" of human experience. This brand of "aesthetic" Marxism in the 1930s was described as **Critical Theory**, and agreed on certain principles of social investigation.

Opposition to **positivism** in the social sciences.

Opposition to dogmatic, crudely materialist **Stalinism**.

Only a **permanently self-critical** approach to theory can avoid paralysis.

Critical Theory represented a "negative" libertarian alternative to the empires of Soviet Communism and US-led capitalism, particularly in the Cold War years of deadlock after 1945, and it influenced the New Left radicalism of the 1960s.

Negative Dialectics

Almost every aspect of Hegel's thinking has been reworked and incorporated in the Critical Theory of T.W. Adorno (1903-69). The result is a **Negative Dialectic**, the title of his chief work. But Adorno, reflecting the experience of the Holocaust and Stalin's totalitarianism, confronts a "bad totality".

Reason itself appears insane as the world acquires systematic totality.

Deconstruction

Jacques Derrida's own project, although not Marxist, is also one of negative dialectics indebted to Hegel as the first "deconstructionist".

My work is a dialectical disentangling — or **deconstruction** — of the webs which thinking itself has spun ever since Plato.

Critical Theory in its "postmodern" form still uses Hegelian methods, but acknowledges a residue of reality which will always escape **total** theorization. Contemporary post-Hegelian dialectics addresses a totalization that is recognized either as "bad" (totalitarianism) or entirely "collapsed" (the end of Grand Narratives).

Alexandre Kojève (1900-68), a Russian emigré, presided over the return to a Marxist-existentialist reading of Hegel. Kojève gave important lectures at the *École Pratique des Hautes Etudes* between 1933 and 1939 (only published after the war in 1947).

It may well be that the future of the world, and thus the sense of the present and the significance of the past, will depend in the last analysis on contemporary interpretations of Hegel's work.

Kojève concentrated almost exclusively on the intellectual drama of Hegel's *Phenomenology*, in particular the life and death struggle described by the "master vs. slave" dialectic.

Some of the key figures of European intellectual life regularly attended Kojève's courses — **Raymond Aron**, **Georges Bataille**, **Jacques Lacan**, **Maurice Merleau-Ponty** and, less frequently, the high priest of Surrealism, **André Breton**.

We, Surrealists, recognize Hegel as one of our own mad company, willing to explore the furthest reaches of Unreason in order to win a new, expanded and higher form of Reason.

And Georges Bataille...

I am closer to Nietzsche than to Hegel, but the fable of the master and the slave is important because it reveals a **complicity** in the relations of power and a struggle for **recognition**.

What attracted Bataille still inspires some contemporary feminist philosophers, such as **Drucilla Cornell** who describes herself as a Left Hegelian.

History is Always Right

The absence of any discussion of the future by Hegel was unacceptable to the next generation of "Young Hegelians". Hegel's retrospective **historicism** had to be transmuted into historical **futurism**.

The danger is that Hegel's logic could be twisted to justify anything that happens in history.

Hegel believed that he had revealed the rule of Reason in the unfolding of Spirit through world history. But this carries the unfortunate implication that whatever has been successful is thereby also somehow "right" and superior to what has been unsuccessful. Whatever vanished from the memory of history, because it was destroyed or unsuccessful, was to Hegel an "unjustified existence".

Charles Darwin (1809-82), like Hegel, also starts from what has been empirically successful and argues back to the supposed necessity of its appearance. In Darwin, however, there is no longer a rational dialectic of nature, but instead a principle of "natural selection". Both Hegel and Darwin can be mis-used to support a belief in the "survival of the fittest".

Seen in the light of such a "Darwinian Hegelianism", world history presents a very ugly spectacle — at its most grotesque in the triumphalism of the Nazis.

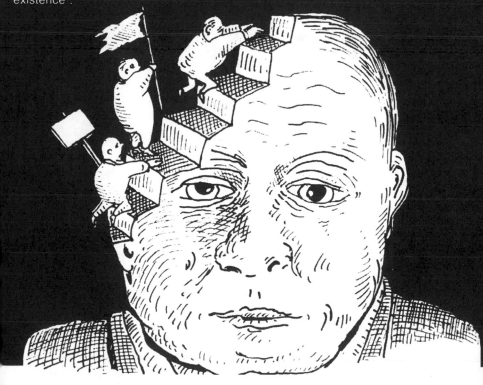

Fukuyama's "End of History"

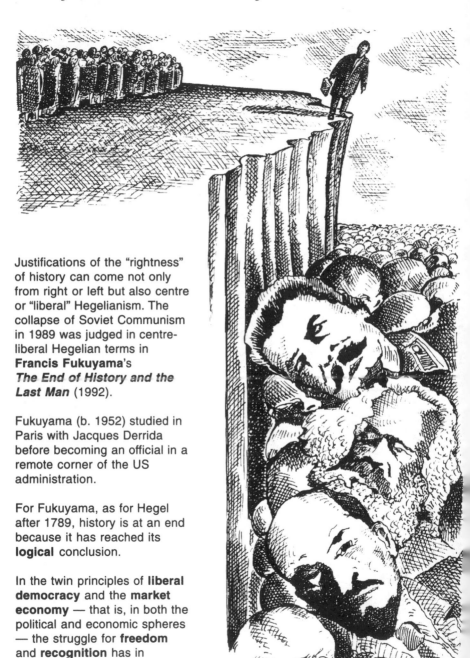

Justifications of the "rightness" of history can come not only from right or left but also centre or "liberal" Hegelianism. The collapse of Soviet Communism in 1989 was judged in centre-liberal Hegelian terms in **Francis Fukuyama**'s *The End of History and the Last Man* (1992).

Fukuyama (b. 1952) studied in Paris with Jacques Derrida before becoming an official in a remote corner of the US administration.

For Fukuyama, as for Hegel after 1789, history is at an end because it has reached its **logical** conclusion.

In the twin principles of **liberal democracy** and the **market economy** — that is, in both the political and economic spheres — the struggle for **freedom** and **recognition** has in principle been won.

Fukuyama's case for the world triumph of liberal free enterprise seems an over-optimistic vindication of American capitalist imperialism. Since the publication of his book, Fukuyama has explained that he is actually quite pessimistic and is trying to educate his public in the Hegelian logic of his interpretation.

What I do claim is that liberal democracy is now the only **universalistic** ideology in play.

Profound and urgent political issues at stake here have been discredited by Fukuyama's superficial treatment of them. For the first time in history, all forms of universalism seem discredited or on the defensive. What remain are the particularisms of "private interest" and (the "bad infinity" of) "freedom of choice", nationalism and religious fundamentalism. A new capitalist fundamentalism claims to have swept all appeals to humanity or to any larger ideals into the dustbin of history.

In Conclusion

What can we gain from understanding Hegel today? By now, the answer should be evident. For the last 150 years, almost every major development in philosophy from Marx to Derrida and postmodernism can be seen as confronting the challenge of Hegel's system. Nor is Hegel's influence confined to philosophy only — it has had dramatic consequences in the spheres of political ideas and politics itself worldwide.

In short, we cannot know **where** we are now without recognizing Hegel as our original point of departure.

"Philosophy always comes on the scene too late to give instruction as to what the world ought to be. As the **thought** of the world, it appears only when actuality is already there, cut and dried, after its process of formation has been completed... When philosophy paints its grey on grey, then a shape of life has grown old. It cannot be rejuvenated by philosophy's grey on grey; it can only be understood. It is only with the fall of dusk that the owl of Minerva spreads its wings."

Hegel, *Philosophy of Right*

Further Reading

Hegel's Own Writings

Hegel's best writing is often offered in the introductions and prefaces he wrote to his various works. They often draw together the main themes and offer brilliant illustrations or metaphors to make his intention clear.

There are three excellent collections of thematically organized extracts edited by Walter Kaufmann, Michael J. Inwood and Frederick G. Weiss, respectively.

Hegel's most succinct statement of his philosophical system is given in his Encyclopaedia of the Philosophical Sciences. Its three volumes were published in English translation by Oxford University Press as:
Part I: the Logic, trans. W. Wallace (1975)
Part II: the Philosophy of Nature, trans. A.V. Miller (1970)
Part III: the Philosophy of Mind, trans. W. Wallace (1971)

The Phenomenology of Spirit is available in a splendid edition from Oxford University Press (Oxford and New York, 1977) translated by A.V. Miller. It comes with a paragraph by paragraph commentary on the text and a very good foreword by J.N. Findlay.

There are English language editions of Hegel's Science of Logic, his lectures on Aesthetics, Religion, the History of Philosophy and the Philosophy of World History. Hegel's Philosophy of Right (trans. H. B. Nisbet, Cambridge University Press, 1991) is available in a splendid new edition edited by Allen Wood with an excellent introduction and apparatus. Many of Hegel's long lecture courses have not only been translated in full but, because of Hegel's habit of offering a kind of summary in his introductions, these have also been published separately.

Biography

There are very few English language sources for Hegel's life. Franz Wiedmann's Hegel (translated from the German, Pegasus, New York, 1968) is a straightforward chronological treatment of his life. Walter Kaufmann's Hegel: a Reinterpretation (University of Notre Dame Press, Notre Dame, Indiana, 1978) includes lots of biographical detail and a collection of documents (extracts from the letters, contemporary accounts and so on). The voluminous correspondence is translated by C. Butler and C. Seiler as Hegel: The Letters (University of Indiana, Indianapolis, 1984). It is thematically organized with masses of editorial information about Hegel's life, his works and his friends and contemporaries.

Books on Hegel

Each of the following attempts to offer an introduction to Hegel's thought from a particular perspective.

Hegel and Marx, Elie Kedourie (This is probably the best all-text introduction to Hegel; Marx is only treated in one chapter in relation to Hegel.) (Blackwell, Oxford UK and Cambridge USA, 1995)
Hegel, Peter Singer (Oxford Past Masters, Oxford University Press, Oxford and New York, 1983)
Hegel, Clark Butler (Twayne World Authors, Twayne, New York, 1977)
Hegel and Modern Society, Charles Taylor (Cambridge University Press, Cambridge and New York, 1979)
The Philosophy of Hegel, G.R.G. Mure (Thoemmes Press, London, 1993 reprint of 1965 edition)

Other excellent books about Hegel which offer clear, well-written treatments.

Hegel, Charles Taylor (Cambridge University Press, Cambridge and New York, 1975)
The Spirit of the Phenomenology, R.C. Solomon (Oxford University Press, Oxford and New York, 1983)
Hegel's Theory of the Modern State, Shlomo Avineri (Cambridge University Press, Cambridge and New York, 1972)
Beauty and Truth: A Study of Hegel's Aesthetics, Stephen Bungay (Oxford University Press, Oxford and New York, 1986)

Dedication

To Annie

I first read Hegel with Mark Newman and Dorian Yeo in 1975. Dorian read through this manuscript, too, and offered many helpful comments. My part of this book is in memory of Rick Turner and the spirit of '75.

Thanks to the three friends already mentioned and to Pam, Tony, Mike, Michael, Adrienne, Andy and everyone else who was there or thereabouts in '75. Thanks, too, to my parents (for their help and understanding in '75) and to Ann, Michael and Nikki (for their help and understanding in '95).

Lloyd

Artist's Acknowledgements

The illustrator wishes to thank Basia, Malgosia and Kola for their help, without which this book would never have come into existence.

Biographies

Lloyd Spencer is Senior Lecturer in the School of Media at Trinity and All Saints, University College, Leeds.

Andrzej Krauze is an illustrator who publishes regularly in *The Guardian*, the *New Statesman & Society* and *The Sunday Telegraph*.

Designed by **Andrzej Krauze** and **Zoran Jevtic**.

Index